AMERICAN LABOR

FROM CONSPIRACY
TO
COLLECTIVE BARGAINING

THE KNIGHTS
OF ST. CRISPIN
1867-1874

Don D. Lescohier

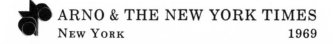 ARNO & THE NEW YORK TIMES
NEW YORK   1969

Reprint edition 1969 by Arno Press, Inc.

Library of Congress Catalog Card No. 77–89748

Reprinted from a copy in
The State Historical Society of Wisconsin Library

Manufactured in the United States of America

THE KNIGHTS
OF ST. CRISPIN
1867-1874

BULLETIN OF THE UNIVERSITY OF WISCONSIN

NO. 355

ECONOMICS AND POLITICAL SCIENCE SERIES, VOL. 7, No. 1, PP. 1-102.

THE KNIGHTS OF ST. CRISPIN, 1867–1874

A STUDY IN THE INDUSTRIAL CAUSES OF TRADE UNIONISM

BY

DON D. LESCOHIER

Special agent, Minnesota Bureau of Labor, Industries and Commerce

MADISON, WISCONSIN

MAY, 1910

CONTENTS

THE KNIGHTS OF ST. CRISPIN, 1867–1874[1]

A STUDY IN THE INDUSTRIAL CAUSES OF TRADE UNIONISM

CHAPTER I

HISTORICAL SKETCH

The Knights of St. Crispin, a national organization of shoemakers, was the largest of the many national labor unions that flourished during the ten years that followed the Civil War.[2] This union was organized on March 1, 1867 at Milwaukee, Wisconsin,[3] by Newell Daniels, formerly of Milford, Massachusetts, and six associates.[4] During the spring the German Cus-

---

[1] The author desires to express his deep indebtedness to Dr. John B. Andrews, Executive Secretary of the American Association for Labor Legislation, who collected for the American Bureau of Industrial Research most of the materials out of which this study was constructed, and to Professor John R. Commons, of the University of Wisconsin, in whose Research Class in Labor and Industry this study began. Without the inspiration, guidance and criticism of Professor Commons this record had never been written.

[2] The name was chosen by F. W. Wallace of Milwaukee, one of the Charter members. St. Crispin was the patron saint of shoemakers. According to tradition he and his brother, St. Crispinian, lived in the third century A. D. Born pagans, they were converted to Christianity and travelled through France preaching the gospel. They supported themselves on their journeys by making shoes. They met martyrdom at the hand of Recitus Varrus, governor under Maxmillian Hercules, on October 25, 287 A. D.

[3] In the factory of Atkins, Steele and White. A. H. Atkins of this firm and his son H. L. Atkins, who was employed in his father's factory, at the time the Crispins started, now reside in Madison, Wisconsin, where they are still engaged in shoe manufacture. These gentlemen have contributed very materially both to this history of the Knights of St. Crispin and to our analysis of the industrial situation.

[4] The charter members were Newell Daniels, Samuel Wilson, W. C. Haynes, F. W. Wallace, Al. Jenkins, C. Houren and Henry Palmer. Daniels was a boottreer by trade and while at Milford had planned to form a national organization

tom Shoemakers' Union of Milwaukee took the Crispin form of organization and in September Daniels established lodges in Oswego, New York, and Milford, Hopkinton and Stoughton Center, Massachusetts. The Chicago Shoemakers' Union of over six hundred members joined the order in January, 1868,[5] making seven Crispin lodges, four in the East and three in the West.[6]

The development during the next three years was rapid. Eighty-seven lodges were formed before the first meeting of the International Grand Lodge at Rochester, New York, July 1, 1868,[7] two hundred and four (204) before the second, Boston, April, 1869;[8] three hundred and twenty-seven (327) before the third, Boston, April, 1870;[9] and nearly four hundred (400) before the fifth, Boston, April, 1872.[10] In the twenty-seven months between January 1, 1868 and April 1, 1870, three hundred and twenty (320) lodges were organized, an average of a new lodge every two and one-half days for a period of two and one-fourth years.

The location of the new lodges established each year is significant.[11] Most rapid development occurred where industrial conditions were worst. The order started in Milwaukee and did not enter the East until September 1867, but seventy of the one hundred and twenty-five (125) lodges established during 1867 and 1868 were in Massachusetts and thirty in other parts of the East. The other twenty-five were in the larger cities of Wisconsin, Illinois, Ohio, Michigan, Missouri, and Canada;

---

of boot-treers. His removal to Milwaukee delayed his plans, and more mature reflection convinced him that instead of a trade organization an industrial union including all shoe workers was needed. *K. O. S. C. Monthly Journal,* Jan. 1873. Article by Newell Daniels.

[5] Gavin had been the secretary of the Chicago Union. He later became a national leader of the Crispins.

[6] The early history here given is taken from the report of Newell Daniels to the first Grand Lodge, Rochester, New York, July 1868, and from the proceedings of the Grand Lodges of 1869, 1870 and 1872. Daniels' Rochester report was published in the *K. O. S. C. Monthly Journal* Jan., 1873. A brief historical sketch may be found in Frank Foster's article in McNeill's *Labor Movement,* pages 192-213.

[7] *Proceedings,* 1869, p. 6.

[8] *Proceedings,* 1869, pp. 6, 7.

[9] *Proceedings,* 1870, p. 16.

[10] *Proceedings,* 1872, p. 48. The fourth Grand Lodge was held at New York, April 1871 and the sixth at Cleveland, April 1873.

[11] An Official List of Lodges published by the International Grand Lodge on December 1, 1870, is the source of the facts of the four succeeding paragraphs.

notably Chicago, Cincinnati, Cleveland, Detroit, Milwaukee, St.
Louis and Montreal. Forty-three of the one hundred and fifty-
five (155) organized during 1869 were in Massachusetts, twenty-
one in New York, and forty-seven in other parts of the East.
Columbus, Indianapolis, Louisville, San Francisco, Grand
Rapids (Michigan) and many smaller cities were added to the
western group and Toronto, St. Johns, Quebec, Guelph, Hamil-
ton, and Windsor to the Canadian. The distribution of the
lodges established during 1870 was distinctly different. Four-
fifths of them were in the West, and, for the most part, in small
cities. Michigan organized eleven, Wisconsin and Indiana seven
each, Canada eight, and other western states smaller numbers.

The period of rapid growth ended in December, 1870. At that
time Massachusetts had eighty-five active lodges; New York,
forty-seven; Pennsylvania, about a dozen; New Hampshire, fifteen; New Jersey, eight: Michigan, fifteen; Ohio, fourteen; Indiana, thirteen; Wisconsin, ten; Illinois, seven; and Canada,
seventeen.[12]

The districts where lodges were formed most rapidly were
also those in which they strove most earnestly and persisted
most stubbornly. The great strikes were in the shoe centers
early organized—Lynn, Worcester, Philadelphia, Chicago. At
the sessions of the Grand Lodge the lodges first established had
the larger representation. Local lodges number 1 to 100 sent
eighty-five delegates to the Grand Lodge of 1869, while lodges
101 to 204 sent only fifty-two.[13] Less than fourteen per cent
of the lodges organized during 1867 and 1868 were decadent on
December 1, 1870, though twenty-four per cent of the two hundred and thirty established during 1869 and 1870 had already
perished.

The exact membership attained by the Knights of St. Crispin
is not known. *The Hide and Leather Interest* estimated it in
May, 1869, at from thirty thousand to sixty thousand.[14] Frank
Foster thought it reached only forty thousand,[15] though the

---

[12] *Official List of Lodges*, Dec. 1, 1870.
[13] *Proceedings*, 1869, pp. 31, 32.
[14] *American Workman*, Boston, June 5, 1869.
[15] *McNeill, G. E., The Labor Movement*, p. 200.

Massachusetts' Crispins alone claimed that many.[16] The *New York Tribune* declared in May 1869 that there were then eighteen thousand Crispins in and around New York and fifty thousand in the United States.[17] The organization's records show that about four hundred lodges were established, many of which had over six hundred members,[18] and some over a thousand. Unity Lodge of Lynn had over twelve hundred[19] and a Philadelphia lodge over fifteen hundred members. This would indicate that Foster's estimate was a little too low. Even if the maximum number of active lodges never exceeded two hundred and fifty and their membership averaged only two hundred the enrollment would have been fifty thousand.

This was the largest membership attained by any American labor union before 1875. The coopers and cigarmakers in 1871 and 1872 had but twelve thousand members each, the machinists and blacksmiths together but eighteen thousand. The miners, the first union to equal the Crispins in numbers, reached the forty thousand mark in 1875.

The greatest strength of the Knights of St. Crispin was attained between April, 1868, and April, 1871. In this period they won a large proportion of their strikes, successfully resisted many hostile moves on the part of their employers and obtained for themselves the best wages that they had had since the war. Foster speaks of them as being at this time the most powerful labor organization in the world,[20] while the editor of

---

[16] *American Workman*, March 5, 1870.

[17] *American Workman*, May 29, 1869.

[18] *Proceedings*, 1872.

[19] *Workingman's Advocate*, March 30, 1872.

[20] "For five subsequent years after the Rochester session of 1868, the Order of the K. O. S. C. was a power in the land. It made and unmade politicians; it established a monthly journal; it started coöperative stores; it fought, often successfully, against threatened reductions of wages and for better returns to its members for labor performed; it grew rapidly in numbers and became international in scope; it is estimated that 400 lodges and 40,000 members at one time owed it allegiance; it became the undoubted foremost trade organization of the world." McNeill, G. E. *The Labor Movement*, p. 200.

"The K. O. S. C. is one of the most powerful trade organizations in this country. Although but about eighteen months in existence, the several Lodges in the Eastern, Western, and Southern States number, in the aggregate, about fifty thousand men, of which there are about eighteen thousand in this city and vicinity." *New York Tribune*, quoted, *American Workman*, May 29, 1869.

the *Hide and Leather Interest,* an employers' paper, wrote in May, 1869:

"It is well known that the Crispins number from thirty thousand to sixty thousand—we eannot give the exact figures—and have the most perfect organization that it is possible for a trade society to have, its ramifications extending all over the country, the Crispins of Chicago and San Francisco working in perfect harmony with those of Massachusetts."

"Speaking of a strike then waged in Chicago, he continued:

"As soon as the Crispins of Chicago have got things as they want, they will, of course, be in a position to aid those of Massachusetts and then the employers will find out the policy of being beaten in detail."

The editor urged the employers to form a national organization against the Crispins and to import Chinese, French, French-Canadians, Swedes, Germans, or other foreigners as strike breakers.[21]

The decline of the Crispins began in 1871, and it was particularly rapid after the crushing defeat of the Lynn lodges in 1872. Throughout the country growth was hindered from the first by rash strikes, and in some sections, especially Maine and Canada, many lodges were in precarious condition as early as the spring of 1870.[22] The discussion at the Grand Lodge of 1870 showed much dissatisfaction, and in 1871 the officers were changed. William J. McLaughlin, of Ashland, Massachusetts, who had been International Grand Sir Knight since his election at the first Grand Lodge, June, 1868, was replaced by Thomas Ryan of New York, and Newell Daniels, Grand Scribe since March 1, 1867, was succeeded by Samuel P. Cummings of Lynn, Massachusetts. The changes were very unfortunate. Ryan, on charges preferred by Lodge No. 69, of New York, at the session of 1872 was deposed from his office and expelled from the Grand Lodge, while Cummings was denounced by John Dormer of St. Louis, Missouri, for neglect of duty because he had not sent out his quarterly reports. Cummings said in defence of himself that if he had sent out his quarterly reports, the order would have been so discouraged that it certainly would have disbanded in despair. The membership had fallen to about thirteen

---

[21] *American Workman,* June 5, 1869.
[22] *Proceedings,* 1870, p. 19.

thousand,[23] and the attendance at the Grand Lodge had fallen
from one hundred and thirty-three lodges in 1869 to only fifty-
two in 1872.[24]

The officers were again changed in 1872. James R. Wright,
of Baltimore, Maryland, was elected International Grand Sir
Knight, and M. P. Murphy International Grand Scribe. Their administration failed equally with the others to stem the ebbing tide.
Dissatisfaction, insubordination and dissension continued to increase until the sixth annual session (Cleveland, June 1873)
"revealed a deplorable spirit of discord and distrust existing
in the organization." The convention vainly tried to find
means of holding the order together. Delegates proposed coöperation, arbitration, and other plans for unification, but
nothing adequate could be discovered.

The subsequent year witnessed rapid decay, and when the
seventh Grand Lodge met at Philadelphia in June 1874, the
few delegates who were present attended, as one of them told
Frank Foster, "the funeral of the K. O. S. C."[25]

Between 1874 and 1878 a desultory struggle was maintained.
In 1875 G. B. Scully, of Lynn, Massachusetts, made a vigorous effort to revive the order, and succeeded after a year's hard
work in reestablishing it in about thirty towns, mostly in
Massachusetts.[26] The movement was strong enough to defeat
an "iron-clad" contract proposed by the Lynn manufacturers
in 1877 and aroused the hopes of many that the Knights of
St. Crispin would be restored to their earlier power. Mr.
Charles Litchman, Grand Scribe, wrote to the *Workingman's
Advocate* of Chicago in Oct. 1877. "We seem to be upon the
eve of the immediate reorganization of our craft throughout
America. Our International Lodge is in grand condition
financially, every debt being paid, or what is equivalent, money
enough in the treasurer's hands to pay all outstanding bills.
The per capita tax for this quarter is only one half of what it
was last quarter, and will provide ample funds for the expenses
of the next three months. New lodges are constantly being re-

[23] *Proceedings*, 1872, p. 17.
[24] *Proceedings*, 1869, pp. 31, 32; *id.* 1872, pp. 47, 48.
[25] McNeill, G. E., *The Labor Movement*, p. 201.
[26] Chapter VII is a detailed discussion of this movement.

organized outside of this state. All, therefore, that is necessary to make secure this success seemingly within our reach is a little earnestness among the lodges already organized in Massachusetts, and the arousing of the towns not yet with us."

The attempt to revive the order did not, however, attain any considerable success. Something over thirty lodges were established and a few thousand members enrolled, but hardly any influence was obtained outside of Massachusetts. Only twenty-four delegates attended the convention of 1878, twenty-two of whom were from thirteen Massachusetts towns, and the other two from Chicago and Rochester.

Many causes contributed both to the rise and the fall of the Knights of St. Crispin. The order was the product and the victim of complex industrial forces. Changes in markets, in mechanical methods, in the organization of industry, and in the supply of labor, all played their part in inciting its formation and undermining its power. These changes and their effects form the subject of the succeeding chapters.

CHAPTER II

INDUSTRIAL ORGANIZATION AND METHODS OF MANUFACTURE 1860–1872

Business organization and methods of manufacture in the shoe industry at the outbreak of the Civil War differed only in minor details from those of twenty years before. From the standpoint of the labor movement, five types of establishments were engaged in manufacture; custom, custom-retail, sale, "garret" (sweat shop), and merchant capitalist.[1] The early sixties added the factory.

The custom shops had their origin in the eighteenth century when father and son, with perhaps an apprentice or journeyman, pursued their labors in a shop not much larger than an ordinary hen-coop, with a chimney in one corner and a cutting board in another. When a sufficient number of pairs were completed, the boss trudged off to Boston with them in a bag on his shoulders,[2] and sold them either to individual customers, who had left orders, or to merchants. The accumulation of a little capital enabled the boss to employ three or four journeymen, establish a shop outside his home, and develop a regular custom trade.

Except for the use of simple hand and foot-power devices, the manufacturing in these shops was entirely done by hand. The uppers were cut and sent out to women in their homes to stitch and bind, except in the case of such heavy work as the rivermen's boots made at Milwaukee and Chicago. On these

---

[1] The custom, sale and garret shops might be considered by those interested only in manufacturing methods as but one type. The best exposition of the historical development of the various kinds of shops is that by Professor John R. Commons in "American Shoemakers, A Sketch of Industrial Evolution," *Quar. Jour. Econ.*, Nov. 1909.

[2] *Lynn Record*, Feb. 1, 1837.

the upper sewing, as well as the bottoming, had to be done by men. The finished uppers, together with the stock for the bottoms (vamp, sole, insole, slip and heel leather) and the lasts, made, in the case of the custom shop, to the order of the customer, were given to a team of journeymen to "make."[3] A team consisted of one or two lasters, a heel shaver, an edge maker, a tacker-on, and a stone and black-ball man. The latter, who gave a smooth finish to the soles, was not included in teams making rough work.[4]

The distinguishing peculiarity of these custom shops was their market. They sold to individual customers at prices fixed by individual bargains and were able both to get the highest prices and pay the highest wages. An important modification of the custom shop, from this point of view, was the custom-retail shop. It carried a small stock of ready made shoes on which it competed directly with retail merchants. The essential difference between custom and retail prices, namely, that custom prices are fixed by individual bargains with customers more anxious for quality and fit than for cheapness while retail prices are fixed by market competition, compelled a double scale of prices and of wages in the custom-retail shop, one for custom and one for shop work. A shoe of given quality commanded a different price and afforded a different wage when sold at custom than when sold at retail. Thus appeared the anomaly of the same men receiving at different times (perhaps on the same day) different rates of wages on the same grade of work.[5] Dissatisfaction naturally resulted. When the shops were large enough to employ separate groups of journeymen on custom and on shop work the irritation was continuous. The New York State Lodge took active steps in 1870 to stop the practice in that state because

---

[3] Stores handling shoe makers' supplies carried what were called "custom lasts." These were rough lasts, a little undersized, which the custom boss could purchase and "leather up." i. e., pad up, to the exact measurement of his customer. The perfected last was then kept in stock marked with the customer's name.

[4] At Brockton such teams made 108 pairs of shoes a week.

[5] Shop work was paid 50c a pair less than custom work at Chicago. *Workingman s Advocate*, June 22, 1872. After the machine shoes came in many custom-retail shops manufactured only their custom shoes and carried machine shoes for their retail stock.

they found that the lower wages of shop work tended to draw down the wages for custom work.[6]

Midway between the custom-retail and the merchant-capitalist establishments described below were the sale shops. They constituted the next step in the evolution of an individual enterprise from a small to a large scale business. The custom trade was entirely dropped and the business was devoted to supplying a retail, or a retail and wholesale trade.[7] The manufacturer no longer worked at the bench as he had done in the custom and custom-retail stages but gave his whole time to the merchant employer side of the business. The size of his salesroom was increased and he hired journeymen to take materials to their homes for manufacture. Frequently he bought boots and shoes for his counters from the garret bosses (described below) or from wholesale jobbers, and often he sold to the jobbers surplus products manufactured by his journeymen. Thus he tended more and more to become a wholesaler buying raw materials in large quantities, manufacturing them in outside shops and selling them to retail dealers or jobbers.

The merchant-capitalist was concisely described by the *Lynn Record* of January 1, 1834. They were "the shoe merchants or shoe dealers who purchase materials in large quantities and employ many males and females in the various branches of the manufacture, and sell the article wholesale." The details of their method of manufacture were outlined by the Lynn Directory of 1851.[8]

"The stock for the shoes is cut in the larger buildings, called manufactories, [i. e. the merchant-capitalist's warehouse], by men termed clickers. The upper parts are then tied in packages and given to females, who reside at their own homes, to be bound. They are then returned to the manufactories, where they are put together in bundles with the soles, and distributed to the workmen who make the shoes in small—quite too small—shops, usually at or near their homes. . . . When the shoes are finished, they are packed at the manufactories in wooden boxes,

---

[6] *Proceedings*, 1870, p. 16.
[7] Lodge 26, Knights of St. Crispin, Detroit, Mich., was composed entirely of workmen in these shops. *American Workman*, Sept. 18, 1869.
[8] Quoted by Johnson, D. N. *Lynn, Fifty Years a City*, p. 178.

usually containing about sixty pairs, and sent to all places where there is a demand for them.''

Two methods for giving out the work to journeymen and binders (women) were in common use by merchant-capitalists during the thirty-five years preceding the war, and both methods were frequently employed by the same firm.[9] In the one case the journeyman came to the warehouse and received enough work to last him a week, which he manufactured either at his own home, alone or assisted by a journeyman or apprentice, or in small shops, working coöperatively with fellow journeymen. In the other case, the work was given out to contractors who then subcontracted it at piece prices to journeymen working at home or in teams in the contractors' shops.[10] There seems to have been a steady development of this contract or sweating system from 1840 to 1870,[11] and when the factories came it was carried into them. Foremen were given contracts for the work in their departments, and made their own earnings by the margin between the contract price that they received and the wage cost of manufacturing.

The sweatshops, like the custom shops, developed out of the small shops of the early nineteenth century.[12] These were commonly about twelve feet square and owned by a ''boss'' who employed from four to eight journeymen and one or two apprentices—''boys on the seam.''[13] The stock manufactured belonged to the boss, and the product was sold either at custom, at retail, or at wholesale to local merchants. After the merchant-capital-

---

[9] For instance, at Worcester there were large merchant-capitalist firms that supplied work to shoemakers in Worcester and the neighboring small towns. Some of the journeymen in the small towns and most of those in Worcester took work in the first manner described, many of those in the outlying towns through contractors. *American Workman*, Hearing on Massachusetts Lodge Incorporation bill, April 1870. (Illustrated in several issues.)

[10] *American Workman*, as above.

[11] It developed with the same evils as those characteristic of sweating in other industries—long hours, low wages, and speeding up. The hours in these shops between 1840 and 1860 were frequently from 14 to 16 and the wages often as low as $5.00 a week.

[12] Side by side with the shops were the thousands of journeymen who had their little shops in their homes and manufactured with the help of their family, an apprentice, or a hired journeyman.

[13] Johnson, D. N., *Sketches of Lynn*, pp. 23-70, has the best description that I have seen of these early shops.

ists organized the manufacture on a larger scale and offered to employ the small shops to work up their raw materials, many bosses stopped independent manufacturing and contracted to manufacture for the capitalists. The profits of the boss then changed from profits on capital to profits on laborers and the character of the boss from merchant-employer to contractor-employer. Instead of his gains depending upon shrewdness in buying and selling or skill in manufacturing, they now depended upon the exploitation of workmen. The merchant-capitalists played the contractors against each other to reduce prices; the contractors played the workmen against each other to reduce wages. Each reduction in wages by individual capitalists, since it gave those effecting the reduction a competitive advantage, tended to register itself in the general wages of journeymen.

Similar in its effect upon wages was the competition of the garret boss. He differed from the sweatshop boss in only one respect; he owned the raw materials and the products. But, like the sweatshop boss, he was a price-cutter. He sold his products "to jobbers and retailers in small quantities at low rates for cash." He undercut both prices and wages, and got his earnings, not like the custom manufacturer, from profits on goods sold, but like the sweat-shop contractor, from the exploitation of labor. The severity of his competition is illustrated by the situation in Philadelphia, where in 1858 a single retailer bought fifteen thousand dollars worth of shoes from the garret bosses.[14]

The fundamental differences between the effects of custom, custom retail, sale, garret, sweatshop, and merchant-capitalist employment upon the welfare of the shoemaker are now apparent. Though they all used the same hand methods of manufacture, the same team work and labor-saving devices, and the same division of labor between males and females, each had a different influence upon wages. The character of the influence in each case was determined by the market supplied. The custom shops, because their selling prices were fixed by individual bargains, could adapt prices to wages and pay their men at the highest rates. Retail manufacturers, since they saved jobber's

---

[14] Freedley, E. T., *Philadelphia and its Manufactories*, (1858) p 188.

profits and transportation expense, were in the second grade
of advantage. Wholesale manufacturers, whether merchant-
capitalists, sweatshop contractors, or garret bosses, had to meet
the competition of the cheapest wholesale producers and to
adapt wages to wholesale prices.

The competition of contract labor in prisons, and of the French
Canadians, who came down into New England during the busy
season and returned at its close, constituted additional wage de-
pressing forces. The effect of prison labor is best shown by an
illustration. Messrs. Whitney, Yundt & Whitney, of Chicago,
bid sixty-two cents a day for the labor of the two hundred and
fifty convicts in an Illinois penitentiary.[15] The shoes manufactured were sold on the open market. New York, Maryland and
other states had a similar penal policy and honorable manufacturers and honest workmen were compelled to compete with
sixty-two cent convicts.

The French Canadian competition was disastrous in two ways.
In the first place, the Canadians worked at the lowest of wages,
because they could return to their fishing and farming when
"the season" was over. In the second place, they increaased
the labor supply to such an extent that they prevented the journeymen from forcing wages up at the only time in the year
when they were in a position to enforce their demands.

The five systems of manufacture thus far mentioned that existed in 1851 all employed hand methods. The machine era had
not yet begun. The first step toward a factory system came with
the invention in 1846 and utilization in 1852 of a sewing machine
for stitching uppers. The invention of labor saving devices had
begun in 1810 with a clumsy lasting and nailing machine,
and had been very active during the thirties and forties, but had
produced nothing adequate for the equipment of factories.[16]
The most that had been attained were such hand and foot-power
labor-saving devices as tin patterns for assistance in cutting up-

---

[15] *Workingman's Advocate,* August 25, 1871.
[16] Shaler, N. S., *United States of America,* Vol. II, Chap. 3, p. 182, cites 13
kinds of splitting machines, 18 devices and processes for making, 16 for pegging
and nailing, 4 for lasts, 15 for crimping boot fronts, 5 for rolls to harden soles,
3 for clamps and pricking devices for hand sewing, 17 for cutting, 3 for
benches, 2 for lasting tools, 4 for boot-trees, 3 for peg-making.

pers, strippers and sole cutters for blocking out soles, adjust-
able lasts, and the Howe stitching machine referred to above.
The introduction of the stitching machine radically modified the
manufacture of uppers. Much of the work was taken away
from women working at home and given to machine girls working in stitching shops run either by contractors or merchant-
capitalists.[17] It was soon followed by the invention of levellers
and skivers—the first to shape the shoes after they were manufactured, the second to cut the edges of the sole leather. Heel
making, lasting, and sandpapering machines were next invented.
Pegging machines, run by steam power, were introduced in
Lynn and Philadelphia in 1857 and the promise of a factory
system was at hand. A Philadelphian triumphantly declared
that these would "peg two rows on either side of a boot or shoe
in three minutes and cut their own pegs."[18] The same year
saw the invention, by Lyman R. Blake, of Abington, Massachusetts, of the sole sewing machine which, when perfected by Mc-
Kay in 1862, was destined to revolutionize shoe manufacture.
By means of a "horn" which held a thread within the shoe and
a needle that came up through the sole, it sewed a chain stitch
through the upper, insole, and sole. The journeyman, sewing
by hand, had to sew the welt to the upper and then the sole to
the welt. The machine did both at once and made eighty pairs
while the journeyman made one.

Between 1860 and 1870 invention progressed still more rapidly and, under the stimulus of the war, the machines were util-
ized almost as fast as invented. The Townsend and Bean wax
thread machines, wire nail peggers, and new pricking, breast-
ing and heel-trimming machines were invented, the earlier machines were perfected, and all were rapidly put into use.

---

[17] Massachusetts Statistics of Labor, *Report* 1871, p. 609. Johnson, D. N.,
Lynn, Fifty Years a City, p. 179.
[18] Freedley, E. T., *Philadelphia and its Manufactories*, p. 187.

CHAPTER III

INDUSTRIAL CHANGES DURING THE CIVIL WAR, THEIR CAUSES AND THEIR RESULTS

The development of the factory system, which started with the introduction of the power pegging machine at Lynn and Philadelphia, in 1857, was checked by the industrial depression of 1857 and 1860. During the next three years little progress was made. But the outbreak of the war began a period that taxed every means of production to the utmost. The government's purchases sharply increased the demand for sewed shoes; the patriotism of the journeymen sharply decreased the supply of shoemakers. The invention of the McKay machine in 1862 was quickly followed by its introduction into factories. A Lynn editor wrote in 1864,

"Comparatively few people are aware of the quiet steady revolution that is going on in the business of shoemaking, and particularly as that business is conducted in Lynn. Previous to the introduction of the original sewing machines, which are now universally used for the binding and stitching of the uppers, but little or no improvement or even change had been made in the manufacture of shoes. The awl, the bristle and thread, the lapstone and hammer, with plenty of 'elbow grease' were, as they had been for years, the main appliances of the shoemakers, and little was known or thought of labor-saving machinery. After a time, women's nimble fingers were found inadequate to the demand, and sewing machines soon transformed the old-fashioned 'shoe-binder' into a new and more expansive class of 'machine-girls' whose capacity for labor was only limited by the capabilities of the machines over which they presided. Iron and steel came to the aid of wearied fingers and weakened eyes. This was the beginning of the new era, which is destined to produce results big with lasting benefits to our flourishing city.

"It is scarcely 10 years since the first introduction of machinery of any kind into the manufacture of shoes in this city. Everything was done by hand, even to the cutting out of the soles, which was a slow process, and required the expenditure of a large amount of physical force. The introduction of sole-cutting and stripping machines, although used sparingly, was the first indication that a change was to take place in the business of shoemaking; but no one, even ten years ago, would have dared to prophesy that the change was to be so immediate and so great. The rapid progress that has been made during that time, and *especially within the past year or two,* in the introduction of machinery in shoemaking, has been beyond all previous calculation. It may almost be said that handwork has already become the exception, and machinery the rule. The little shoemaker's shop and the shoemaker's bench are passing rapidly away, soon to be known no more among us; and the immense factory, with its laboring steam-engine and its busy hum of whirling wheels, is rising up in their place to change the whole face of things in this ancient and honored metropolis of the 'workers in the gentle craft of leather.'

"The problem as to how best to bring in and concentrate the vast army of men and women employed in the shoe manufacture of Lynn is one that has attracted the attention of many thinking minds among our business men, but it has never been satisfactorily solved until now. Machinery, and particularly the sewing machine,[1] has done in a few short months what years of theorizing and speculation could not do. It has demonstrated that the factory system can be successfully and profitably introduced into the shoe business; in fact, that, with the rapid strides which the business has made within a few years, it is the only system that can be made available for its successful application in future. Of course, the new system is yet in its infancy—the business is yet in a transition state; but the wheels of revolution are moving rapidly, and they never move backward. Operatives are pouring in as fast as room can be made for them; buildings for 'shoe factories' are going up in every direction; the hum of machinery is heard on every hand; old things are passing away, and all things are becoming new."[2]

The Massachusetts Commissioner of Labor Statistics, writing seven years later said:

"Invention has seemed to center about it [the shoe industry] until every phase of the 'Ancient and Honorable Mysterie of Cordwainers' [shoemakers], has disappeared and in its place have come cutters, stock-fitters, lasters, bottomers, machine op-

---

[1] i. e., the McKay machine.
[2] Quoted.—*Fincher's Trades' Review,* March 26, 1864.

erators, beaders, trimmers, edge setters, finishers, etc., etc.—
men who each perform some fractional part of the trade.''[3]

The rapid building of factories and utilization of machinery
during the war period was the fundamental cause of the Crispin movement. It increased the productive powers of the industry beyond what the normal necessities of the shoe market
required. It filled the industry with surplus labor, and it prepared the way for a period of excessive competition between
employers for orders and between laborers for work.

The manufacturing process in the factories did not require
skilled workmen. Journeymen were still needed for cutting
and for certain other hand operations, but common laborers could
run the machines, each of which performed but a small operation.[4] The absence of any shoemakers' organization with apprenticeship rules that hindered the entrance of new hands into
the trade, the plentitude of work in the small shops for the
journeymen, the manufacturers' need for more labor, and the
cheapness of unskilled labor, combined to allow thousands of
"green hands" from the streets and farms and other occupa-
tions to go into the shoe factories.[5] The effect was not felt until
the end of the war brought an industrial reaction. The return
of thousands of journeymen from the war increased the supply
of labor, the stoppage of the government purchases decreased
the demand for shoes. The South American, Mexican, Austra-
lian, West Indian, and Canadian Markets, which had taken all
surplus products before the war, were found to have been lost.

---

[3] Massachusett's Statistics of Labor, *Report* 1871, p. 232.

[4] Massachusetts Statistics of Labor, *Report* 1871, pp. 604, 609. One factory
operative testified that he had served no apprenticeship and another that he had
served one of three months. "Skilled labor has diminished in value since the
introduction of machinery," he suggestively added. "You can put into a shop
a farm laborer from New Hampshire, and in three days he will learn to do a
part. There is comparatively nothing to learn, and so no apprenticeship is
required."   p. 243. "The skilled shoemaker found that the knowledge and experience gained by years of practice gave him little advantage over the green
hand." *Report* 1877, p. 21.

[5] The situation was well described by a correspondent in *Fincher's Trades'
Review*, Nov. 21, 1863, p. 3, chap. 2 : "They are flooding the factories with boys,
to the great injury of those who have served an apprenticeship to the trade; in
fact, doing just what they please without any regard to our interest or rights."
The reference to "boys" should not be taken to mean child-labor. It rather
refers to young men and others who had not yet acquired the trade.

Wages fell, work became irregular. The seasonal character of the industry was intensified. The shoemaker who could secure steady work at decent prices was exceptionally fortunate.[6]

The most pronounced, if not the most important, evil that confronted the shoeworkers after the war was the shortened working year. Newhall, commenting upon the change from the small shops to the factories, says, "the revolution in the mode of manufacture, brought about by the introduction of machinery, has no more marked feature than the division of time into seasons of intense activity followed by seasons of almost perfect quietness. Orders can be so rapidly filled that when few or none are waiting the manufacturer does not work along accumulating a stock in expectancy."[7] The orders which had formerly covered the whole year could now "be filled in six or eight months."[8] Long periods of unemployment were common, especially in winter, and many of the shoemakers had "to work at anything for support."[9] One of them summarized the situation as follows:

"Since the old system of working in little shops was abandoned for that of larger manufactories, there has been a steady diminution in the length of the working season per year. Before the time of factories there would be a steady run of employment for from seven to ten years, only interrupted by commercial depressions or revulsions. The working hours would be from twelve to fifteen. The season for lighting up, was from September 20 to May 20. Since that time there has never been a year of steady work. At first a month only would be lost; now it has got so that we lose over four months' time every year.

---

[6]"Those of us who have watched the current of events for the last 10 years have seen a remarkable and in some respects unnecessary change in the character of the shoe business of the country caused by the late terrible civil war. For years before the war began we were exporting largely of shoes and leather, especially to the South American and Mexican Republics. In that way we got rid of much of our surplus stock and thus secured, in the main, steady work from year to year, undisturbed except by financial revulsions. The war changed all this and the shoe maker who could secure since 1864 steady employment at a decent price was fortunate indeed. So many shoemakers entered the army that the necessities of the country stimulated the invention of machinery so that now the American market can be fully supplied in eight or nine months." *Proceedings,* 1872, p. 18. The same facts are emphasized in *American Workman,* July 3, 1869.

[7] Newhall, J. R., *Lynn Centennial,* p. 62.

[8] *American Workman,* June 19, 1869.

[9] Massachusetts Statistics of Labor, *Report* 1872, p. 271.

The system is worse here [probably Lynn] than elsewhere, because machinery has been more thoroughly introduced.''[10]

Wages were low as well as irregular. The testimony before the Massachusetts Bureau of Labor showed that the majority of shoeworkers were on the margin of dependence and that it was "impossible to buy a home since the factory system came in." [11] Similar conditions obtained in Baltimore,[12] Chicago and San Francisco.[13]

The *Hide and Leather Interest,* in June, 1869, described the situation as follows:[14]

"We know full well that the boot and shoe workmen as a class are, and have been for several years, suffering at certain seasons of the year from a lack of steady employment, and from a rate of wages that can scarcely be called remunerative. That their condition is one that calls for relief, no one that is acquainted with it will deny; a few individuals, favored by peculiar circumstances, have been able to earn at times four, five, and six dollars per day; but for every one who has earned four dollars per day, there have been ten equally deserving workmen who earned less than half that sum. We know of towns where improved tools and the gang system have not been introduced, where intelligent American workmen are unable to earn by twelve hours' labor more than $1.50 per day. Ten years ago, the shoemakers of New England, as a class, were well fed, well clothed, well housed, and had their pockets well supplied with spending money; now they have less surplus money, are more poorly clothed, and are crowding themselves into smaller tenements, while many of them who formerly saw meat and butter daily upon their tables now see those articles there but seldom. During these ten years, their food and family supplies have nearly doubled in prices, while the wages have increased but half. This may be seen by the following figures gathered from shoe manufacturing towns in Massachusetts.

---

[10] The working seasons under the hand work system were from February 1 to December 1, with a heavier rush in the early spring, and from August to October. Different scales of wages were paid on the spring and fall work with an extra cut for the dullness of the season during the summer. Under the factory system a longer winter period of unemployment was followed by a spring rush, summer unemployment and a fall rush. Massachusetts Statistics of Labor, *Report* 1871, p. 243.

[11] *Id.* p. 245, 246, 612, and many other places.

[12] *Workingmen's Advocate,* Feb. 5, 1870.

[13] Same as above, June 12, 1869.

[14] Quoted, *American Workman,* July 3, 1869.

	Retail prices in 1858	Retail prices in 1868
Flour, per bbl...........	$7 50	$15 00
Beef, per lb.	12	25
Codfish	05	10
Butter	22	35
Tea	50	1 20
Coffee	20	44
Sugar	09	16
Molasses	45	90
Soap	08	13
Coal	6 50	10 00

Taking all the articles needed by the shoemaker to support himself and family, and comparing their present prices with the prices of them in 1858, we find the advance is about ninety per cent. In the same section, and during the same period, the advance in the shoemaker's wages have been as follows:

1858—Wages for cutters and shop hands, $1.50 to $2.25. Average $1.75.

1868—Wages for cutters and shop hands, $2.00 to $3.25. Average $2.62.

Increase per day 87 cents. Thus the increase of wages is fifty per cent or half as much more than the wages earned in 1858. The earnings of the bottomers and other hands have only increased about the same proportion.'' [15]

The shoe industry at the end of the war was evidently in a most chaotic condition. Hand and machine labor were competing fiercely for the market; an oversupply of labor was seeking employment. Markets were lessened though factories had become larger and more numerous. Unskilled labor was on the machines. Wages were low and falling, employment irregular and uncertain. Large manufacturers were reducing wages to increase their competitive advantage, small manufacturers to save themselves from bankruptcy. Out of the chaos came the Knights of St. Crispin, the protest of fifty thousand shoemakers against their unfortunate situation.

---

[15] Endorsed by Samuel P. Cummings, Grand Scribe of the Knights of St. Crispin 1871-2, in an article commenting upon the one from which the above is quoted. *American Workman,* July 3, 1869.

CHAPTER IV

THE RELATION OF THE KNIGHTS OF ST. CRISPIN TO THE INDUSTRIAL CHANGES THAT ACCOMPANIED THE CIVIL WAR

The last chapter showed that the journeymen were affected in three ways by the rapid introduction of factories during the Civil War, namely, reduced wages, a shortened working year, and difficulty in obtaining employment. Newell Daniels found the essential cause of this situation to be the employment of the unskilled, or "green hands", in the factories. They reduced the level of competition, crowded the factories during the rush season, and made employment difficult to secure during the dull season. The remedy, he decided, had to be a national union that would not allow "anyone to learn new hands without the consent of the organization." [1]

This diagnosis was the foundation stone of the Knights of St. Crispin. Upon it was built the structure of the order's organization, purposes, and methods. According to it was directed the order's policies. Its acceptance was the "Open Sesame" to membership.

The Crispins did not direct their attack against the factory system, but against the green hands. They discriminated between the machine and the unskilled laborer operating it. The one they accepted; the other they resisted. And this, as Daniels well knew, was the only policy restricting machinery that public opinion would have tolerated.[2] An attempt to prevent the

---

[1] *K. O. S. C., Monthly Journal*, Jan. 1872. Article by Newell Daniels.

[2] It is not likely that Daniels himself would have countenanced an attempt to prevent the use of machinery. Mr. H. L. Atkins of Madison, Wis., in whose factory at Milwaukee Daniels founded the K. O. S. C., said of Daniels during a personal conversation with the writer, "He was a large souled man and would not have countenanced any opposition to machinery. When he came from the East, he had a strong feeling that somehow wealth was not being distributed as

use of new machinery would have brought upon the organization a storm of public indignation.

But the policy of the national organization did not prevent many local lodges from opposing machinery. Their freedom of action in everything but adherence to the "green hand" principle enabled them to adopt many policies locally that were not recognized by the order nationally. At North Adams the Crispins made it cost a manufacturer more to use a lasting machine than to last by hand, and when the pegging machine was introduced two-thirds of them quit.[3] So popular was this opposition to machinery with some lodges that members made it a platform upon which to run for office.[4]

These efforts of local lodges led to the charge made by manufacturers that the national organization was opposed to machinery. The *Hide and Leather Interest* of May, 1869, contained the following:

"They [the Crispins] have endeavored, through paragraphs in sundry papers, to show that they are not opposed to the introduction of new machinery, knowing the prejudicial effect that the admission of such a fact would have upon the minds of the public; but when they make such a statement they state what they know to he absolutely false. It is only a short time since they refused to allow a new lasting machine that was admirably fitted for the purpose for which it was intended to be used, and this refusal was given by authorities of the order, who declined to allow it to be worked at all."[5]

---

it ought to be. The only means he knew of getting a more equitable distribution was by such an order as the Knights of St. Crispin, which would limit the supply of labor."

[3] It should be said in defense of the Crispins that in this particular case two-thirds of the men were French Canadians and did not represent the best type of Crispins, while the manufacturer, Mr. Sampson, was one of the most aggressive and quarrelsome employers in the State of Massachusetts. One of his foremen said of him before the Massachusetts Bureau of Labor: (Massachusetts Statistics of Labor. *Report* 1871. p. 98.) "Mr. Sampson never kept a bargain with me that he ever made." while one of his friends, a manufacturer, told me in a personal conversation that he was a very aggressive and quarrelsome fellow.

[4] "Speaking of dishonest conniving in locals," McLaughlin said in 1870, "I actually know of where the question of opposing the use of machinery has come up 3 or 4 different times just before an election, and it has been used as a lever to hoist them into office, or keep them in for another term." *Proceedings*, 1870, p. 10.

[5] Quoted, *American Workman*, May 29, 1869.

In reply to such charges the organization again and again passed resolutions deprecating all resistance to machinery. The expression of the Massachusetts Grand Lodge in 1869 is typical:

"Resolved, That we do not oppose the introduction of machinery that lightens human toil, or cheapens production, as we believe that just in proportion as the comforts or luxuries of life are cheapened, they are brought more readily within the reach of the laboring classes; and we therefore repel the oft-repeated charges of hostility to labor-saving machinery as the offspring of hostility and ignorance on the part of those who make them, and unjustified by anything done by the order as a whole, or within the scope of its principles and purposes." [6]

A similar resolution met unanimous support at the International Grand Lodge meeting a month earlier.[7]

The views of the Crispins as a whole on the machinery question are probably expressed more correctly by the views of their leader,[8] William J. McLaughlin, than by the actions of such locals as that of North Adams. He said,

"In the cutting up of the trades and the introduction of new and useful machinery our employers have stolen nearly all the advantages arising from them, so that in place of their being a great blessing to the toiling men, women and children of the land, they have used them as engines of oppression, in keeping the people in subjection, so that by their degradation they might be able to promote their own greatness." [9]

The burden of emphasis in this statement is significant. It is not upon the fact that machinery had been introduced, but upon the fact that the employers had "stolen" all the advantages of it by seizing for themselves both the savings due to its productive power and an increment from the wages of their employees. This had been accomplished very largely through the employment of green hands rather than journeymen in the factories.[10]

---

[6] Same as above, May 22, 1869.
[7] *Proceedings*, 1869, p. 17.
[8] Grand Sir Knight (President) of the National Lodge.
[9] *Proceedings*, 1870, p. 13.
[10] It is worthy of notice that shoe machinery did not injure the journeymen by substituting female or child labor. Though many women and children were employed in the factories it was upon the same parts of the work as they had

At least two methods might have been used by the shoeworkers to prevent the usurpation of their "jobs" by the green hands. The first is that which was used by the Typographical Union when the linotype machines were introduced in the early nineties.[11] The Mergenthaler Company which manufactured the machines were selling them to employers during strikes, and furnishing experts to teach unskilled laborers how to run them.[12] The President of the International Typographical Union reached an understanding with the Mergenthaler Company that the printers would not object to the introduction of the machines if the employers would allow the men already in the offices to run them at a reasonable rate of wages and the Mergenthaler Company would refuse to sell the linotypes to employers during strikes. Mr. Donnelly, president of the printers' organization, testifying before the Industrial Commission, said that the introduction of machinery under this agreement had shortened hours and increased wages. The workmen, as well as the employers and consumers, had shared the benefit of a technical progress.

The Crispins could not make any such agreement as this. Loosely organized, inexperienced and widely scattered, they were not prepared to deal constructively with so difficult a question. Decentralized and unstable in organization, they could not inspire the respect of the machinery manufacturers. Could an agreement have been made, their officers had no power to enforce it.[13]

---

done in their homes or the ware houses under the hand system. Between the K. O. S. C. and the women shoe workers, frequently organized as the Daughters of St. Crispin, were the most cordial relations. The International Grand Lodge, K. O. S. C., at its meeting in 1869 resolved "that the International Grand Lodge of the Order of K. O. S. C. tender to those working women who have joined the Order of Daughters of St. Crispin, their hearty sympathy and pledge them our full support in all honest efforts to improve their social or material condition." *Proceedings*, 1869, p. 26. The New York State Lodge passed a similar resolution the following year. *Proceedings*, 1870, p. 14. *The Utica Daily Observer*, July 1, 1871, tells of a delegation from the Daughters of St. Crispin, attending a Crispin meeting and presenting the officers a gavel and bouquets.

[11] U. S. Industrial Commission, vol. 7, p. 276.

[12] This was also done by the shoe machinery manufacturers of the sixties.

[13] A threatened strike against the introduction of the linotype by a local lodge of printers, was promptly headed off by the national officers, who sent union printers to take the places of the strikers. The Crispin national officers never had such power.

The other method was that used by the Crispins, an organization pledged that "no member shall teach or aid in teaching
any part or parts of boot or shoe making, unless this lodge shall
give permission by a three-fourths vote of those present and
voting when such permission is first asked, except to his own
son or a fellow Crispin." [14] The application of the rule is illustrated by a strike at Binghamton, New York, in December, 1869.
The employees of Lester Bros. & Company struck because the
company put "green hands" into the shop and ordered Crispins to teach them. The strike was financially supported by the
International Grand Lodge as a strike for the fundamental principle of the order.[15]

Adherence to this rule against teaching green hands was the
fundamental duty of the Crispin and the following oath was
alleged by the manufacturers to have been taken by all members
of the organization.

"I do solemnly and sincerely pledge myself, my word and
honor as a man, before God and these witnesses present, that
I will not divulge any of the secrets of this Lodge to any one
who I do not know to be a member in good standing, except my
spiritual adviser. I will not make known any of the signs of
recognition or any matter pertaining to the good of the order.
I faithfully pledge myself, that I will not learn, or cause to be
learned, any new hand, any part of the boot and shoe trade,
without the consent of this lodge, and I will do all I can to prevent others from doing the same. I shall consider myself
bound, if any member shall violate this rule to be his enemy,
and will work against his interest in every way possible without
violating the civil law. I further pledge myself that if a member gets discharged from a job of work, because he refuses to
learn a new hand, that I will not take his place, except the
member discharged gives his consent. I also agree to be governed by the will of the members of the order. This pledge, I
agree to keep inviolate, whether I remain a member or not, as
long as the organization stands. So help me God." [16]

The Crispins, through Samuel Cummings, denied that the
oath was used in the Crispin lodges, but it is in such close har-

---

[14] *Constitution* 1869. Article X.
[15] *American Workman,* Dec. 18, 1869. *Proceedings,* 1870.
[16] *Hide and Leather Interest,* May 1869. Quoted, *American Workman,* May
29, 1869.

mony with their constitution, methods of organization and general practices, that we believe that the allegation of the manufacturers was well founded.

Superficially viewed, the Knights of St. Crispin resembled a fraternal society more than a modern trade union. The organization called itself an "order" and was composed of subordinate state, and national "lodges." The International Grand Lodge, which was composed of delegates from the state and subordinate lodges had power to issue state and local charters, amend the national, state, and subordinate lodge constitutions, determine the order's principles and policies, decide all disputes and control all raising and disbursement of money.[17] During the periods between the annual meetings, its powers and duties rested in an Executive Council, composed of the international officers.[18] At each annual meeting this Council was required to give a detailed report of its administration during the preceding year.

The state and local lodges, especially the local, enjoyed a large freedom of action. In everything but obedience to the "green hand" principle and payment of the financial apportionments, the subordinate lodges had complete autonomy. This constituted a fundamental difference between the Knights of St. Crispin and more recent labor unions, which centralize powers of control in their national officers that extend over the entire life of the local unit. Their national organizations take part in the arrangement of trade agreements, boards of arbitration, schedules of hours, and rates of wages, and in the maintenance and settlement of strikes The International Grand Lodge of the Knights of St. Crispin had little to do with any of these questions. It participated in local disputes only when a local lodge struck against either green hands or an effort on the part of manufacturers to break up the lodge. In these cases the local had a "grievance" which entitled it to the financial support of the rest of the order. It was fighting for the fundamental principles of Crispinism.

That Daniels should have made defence of the order and re-

---

[17] *Constitution* 1869, Articles II, VII, XI, XIV and XV.
[18] *Constitution* 1869, Article VI.

sistance to the green hand the only purposes for which the strike funds of the order could be used shows how definitely he purposed that the Crispins should concentrate their efforts upon the permanent solution of their wage problem and not divert and perhaps waste their resources in strikes for local and temporary betterments. Yet this very concentration of effort upon which he based his hopes proved to be one of the causes of failure. Many local lodges could not wait with patience until the limitation of the labor supply should increase wages and make employment regular. They embarked on strikes for immediate relief, and felt that the national officers ought to give them support. So pronounced was this feeling that during 1871 and 1872 many Crispin leaders wanted wage conflicts and trade agreements placed under the control of the national officers.[19] But nothing was done. The organization adhered to the policies of its founders.

The most important function of the Grand Lodge was the financial support of grievances. This formed the very object of its existence. A nation-wide movement against the green hands might have been instituted without a permanent national organization if the local lodges could have won their fights without outside aid. It was the fact that opposition to the green hands meant long periods of unemployment, and sometimes the permanent closing of the employers' shops against the strikers that made a national organization imperative. A central body was needed to raise the necessary funds, determine the legitimacy of requests for them, and distribute them wisely.

Grievances were defined in the International Constitution of 1869 as being discharged for refusing to teach new help, being discharged for belonging to the Crispin organization and being discharged for being conspicuous as a Crispin organizer or advocate.[20] Provision for the investigation of grievances alleged to have been sustained by subordinate lodges[21] was followed in the constitution by a requirement that when a grievance had been recognized by the Grand Lodge the local Scribe should

---

[19] *Proceedings* 1872.
[20] *Constitution* 1870, Article XIV, Sec. 1.
[21] *Constitution* 1870, Article XIV, Sec. 2 and 3.

write to the International Grand Scribe stating the "date of commencement, and names of those out of employment, number of children under 12 years of age, and the amount of money necessary to relieve." [22] The relief was limited to $6.00 a week for a man, $2.00 for his wife and $1.00 for each child under twelve years of age.[23]

Grievance funds were raised by annual contributions of each member to a "contingent fund" held in the treasury of the local lodge, and by special assessments. The state and international grand lodges made requisitions upon these local contingent funds whenever they needed money to assist lodges involved in grievance strikes; the state lodges when the funds were to be used within the state and the national lodge when the funds were to be applied in other states. No lodge could be drawn upon twice or for more than one-half of its contingent fund until all of the lodges had been drawn upon.[24] A system of deputies was depended upon for the enforcement of the requisitions. Section 10 of Article IV of the *Constitution* of 1870 reads as follows:

"Each lodge shall have one deputy, who shall be appointed by the International Grand Sir Knight, through the International Grand Scribe, of the International Grand Lodge, upon the recommendation of the lodge for which he is to act, whose duty shall be to install its officers, receive and communicate the password only to the Sir Knight, or Knight when acting in his absence, collect and forward all taxes levied by the State Province or International Grand Lodges, before installing its officers. All money collected by the deputy shall be at the risk of the Subordinate Lodge, said lodge shall at all times implicitly comply with the orders of said deputy."

The system was not an entire success. Since the deputies were appointed from and practically by the lodges which they served, they were in closer sympathy with the views of the local than of the grand lodge. In many cases they made no effort at all to enforce the decrees of the national officers, and McLaughlin in 1870 feared lest the laxity of the deputies would

---

[22] *Constitution* 1870, Article XIV, Sec. 4.
[23] *Constitution* 1870, Article XIV, Sec. 5.
[24] *Constitution* 1870, Article XIV, Sec. 7.

result in the disintegration of the order.[25] The Grand Lodge of 1871, therefore, added to the Deputy clause in the constitution the following stringent section. "Any deputy failing to comply with the requirements of this Article, shall be deemed guilty of perfidy to the Order and liable to suspension."[26] Had the deputy plan succeeded it would have welded the Knights of St. Crispin into a closely knit organization and made easy the accumulation of grievance funds. Its failure left the order a mere conglomeration of scattered lodges, varying in nationality,[27] work[28] and interest, and made a successful financial system impossible.

The grievances were both many and costly. During 1868, 1869 and 1870 they were sustained by the lodges in New York City, Philadelphia, Boston, Baltimore, Rochester, Albany, Newark, Lynn, Worcester, Milford, Massachusetts, Binghampton, New York, New Haven, New Bedford, Chicago, Detroit, Lansing, Michigan, Milwaukee, Ashland, Wisconsin, Quebec, Montreal, Georgetown, Ontario, Wrentham, Ontario, and many other cities. The cost of few typical cases is shown in the following list:

	Year.	No. of Men.	Cost.	Duration.
Chicago	1869		$35,898 98	Several we'ks
Quebec	1870		3,472 78	9 weeks.
Milford	1870		Very heavy	
Binghamton, N. Y.	1870		585 50	
Georgetown, Ont.	1870	19	745 00	5 weeks.
New Bedford	1870	19	1,300 00	
Worcester	1870	1,200	175,000 00	3 months.

The employers increased the grievance burden by bringing cn disputes in such a manner as to constitute grievances. They

---

[25] See Appendix II.

[26] *Constitution* 1871, Article VII, Sec. 2.

[27] The constitution was printed in French, German and Scandinavian and there were at least 12 German and 3 French besides Scandinavian lodges, composed entirely of the special nationalities.

[28] A large part of the lodges, and frequently all of the lodges in certain towns or districts were composed of men doing a certain type of work, which often differed as much from that done by the members of other lodges as house carpentering does from cabinet making. At Lockport, N. Y., Nashville, Tenn., Milwaukee. Wis., Boston, New York City, and almost all shoe centers were lodges composed entirely of custom workmen. *American Workman*, Feb. 26, 1870, July 24, 1869, Feb. 19, 1870, etc., etc., while in Boston, New York, and all other cities having merchant capitalists were lodges composed of "team men," "cutters," McKay Operators, etc., *American Workman*, Feb. 19, 1870.

thus compelled the national officers to finance at the same time
a number of strikes, none of which they had power to step in
and settle. The frequent requests for grievance funds caused
dissatisfaction among lodges free of disputes, while the inability
of the Grand Lodge to collect the levies involved the national
organization in heavy debts to locals sustaining grievances.[29]
Breaches thus developed between the national officers and local
lodges and confidence in the ability of the organization to carry
out its policies and enforce its demands was undermined.

Inability to finance their grievances was one of the fundamental causes of the failure of the Knights of St. Crispin. Perhaps the task was an impossible one. The very thing that
seemed to be the strength of the order, its size, proved to be
one of its weaknesses. The shoemakers had had no experience
in coöperation on a national scale. They were individualistic,
local. They lacked the sense of common interest, lacked class
consciousness. Differences of nationality made the lack of unity
hard to overcome, and no previous trade union had contributed
guidance from its experience. Even during the first year weaknesses were apparent. In April, 1869, the grand lodge already
owed to various locals grievance funds amounting to over $20,-
000, and the next year the indebtedness was much increased.[30]
At the meeting of the third grand lodge in April, 1870, William
J. McLaughlin said, "The greatest obstacle that the International Grand Lodge has had was that some of the locals were
perfectly indifferent with regard to the payment of the international and grievance taxes. While the Chicago grievance
was going on there were certain persons who discouraged the
lodges from sending in their taxes."[31] At a meeting of the
executive council in the preceding October the principal subject
under discussion had been means of collecting grievance money
from delinquent lodges. Speaking of the discussion, McLaughlin said:

"We knew that we had no power to force these (delinquent)
lodges to pay their taxes. So there was nothing to do but to

---

[29] Grievance strike won in Chicago 1869 and a year later the Grand Lodge
still owed the Chicago Crispins $23, 359. *Proceedings*, 1870, p. 21.
[30] *Proceedings*, 1870, p. 12.
[31] Id., p. 10

ask each member to contribute one dollar or upwards for the purpose of paying our debts; debts that were contracted in fighting our battles. But there has been little money received on that call.''

Daniels, taking up the question in his report said,[32] ''Grievances during the year have been numerous, extensive, and in some cases very destructive to the order, for the reason that they are not promptly and sufficiently supported,—in most cases where there is a grievance the Lodge becomes to a certain extent demoralized and discouraged and is seldom flourishing after. This is one of the most important things to be considered at this meeting. These grievances must be better attended to or we shall soon have no organization. The constitution seems to provide plainly and effectually for grievances, but in its practical operation it must be considered a failure.''

He then moved a tax of $1.00 a member to pay the outstanding debt because, said he, ''Very few of our grievances have been fully paid, which has greatly discouraged the members in those places.'' The report of the Grand Treasurer showed that sixty out of the three hundred and twenty-seven lodges had not paid anything between October 1, 1869 and April 1, 1870. The Crispins failed, even from the first, to finance their grievance strikes adequately, and the failure was fatal. It meant that the free entrance of green hands into the factories could not be prevented by their organization.

Contract labor in prisons and Chinese immigration had the same effect on wages as the green hands. The Crispin efforts to control them were for the most part made by the state lodges rather by an unconscious division of labor than by constitutional provision. The grand lodge was occupied with the support of grievances, the local lodges engrossed with efforts to maintain good wages. The state and province lodges, with but limited power over grievances and no power over wages (until after April 1870), naturally took up the other agitations. In both 1869 and 1870, the New York State lodge conducted a vigorous campaign against contract-labor in prisons. A committee was sent to Albany from the state grand lodge meeting of 1870, and the bill they advocated passed the house with but

---

[32] Id., p. 16.

eleven dissenting votes. It later failed in the Senate.[33] During 1872 the Maryland Crispins had a bill in the Maryland legislature. This also failed. Agitation upon the question was vigorous in all parts of the country but in no case very successful.

Chinese immigration never really affected wages in shoe manufacture except in California, but its fearsome shadow ever fell threateningly across the Crispin pathway. The eastern shoe workers feared that Chinese labor would reduce the cost of manufacture in the West and enable the western manufacturers to wrest the industry from Massachusetts. The western journeymen feared, and with good cause, that the Chinese would drive them from their employment. In 1869, the six hundred Crispins of San Francisco successfully resisted the introduction of Chinese,[34] but in 1871, a thousand were already employed in San Francisco.[35] In 1872 they had monopolized slipper manufacture and forced the Crispin lodge in San Francisco out of existence.[36] In 1879 five thousand of them were at work in San Francisco and eight hundred white shoemakers were walking the streets.[37] The stern logic of events fully justified the fears of the western shoe workers.

Eastern shoe manufacturers, in a convention at Memphis, Tennessee, in 1869, discussed the advisability of introducing Chinese labor into the East,[38] and in December, 1872, Galvin T. Sampson of North Adams, Massachusetts,[39] brought 107 China-

---

[33] *Proceedings*, 1870, pp. 15, 16. As a result of the defeat of the bill the State Lodge passed the following resolution. * * * "*Resolved:* That we, as workingmen, will use our best endeavors to defeat any candidate for office who shall hereafter be placed in nomination by any of the existing political factions who shall so far forget our interests or ignore our rights by not acceding to our just demands that the aforesaid Bill be passed. *Resolved,* That a committee of three be appointed whose duty it shall be to prepare a record of the names of the members of the senate and assembly who shall vote for or against the bill, and have a list of the same printed and posted conspicuously in every workshop and other places of resort throughout the City and State, that workingmen may know to treat 'them, as friends or foes, when they again present themselves as candidates for our suffrage."

[34] *American Workman.* July 24, 1869.

[35] *Workingman's Advocate.* Aug. 5, 1871, p. 3, c. 7.

[36] Same as above.

[37] *National Labor Tribune.* 1879.

[38] *American Workman.* July 31, 1869.

[39] *Workingman's Advocate,* Dec. 21, 1872, p. 2, c. 3.

men from California for his factory. "A high board fence was built about the factory" said a Massachusetts' Crispin to the writer, "and they were kept locked in there. Some of them remained in the East for nearly three years."

The Crispin agitation against the Chinese was continuous, though of course secondary to the agitation against green hands. Covert threats of violence to the Chinese, pleas for legislation and speeches arousing the workingmen, were the characteristic manifestations of hostility. A typical incident was the appearance of Daniel Sheehan of San Francisco and S. P. Cummings of Lynn, Massachusetts, before the Workingmen's Union of New York City, asking for the cooperation of the New York workingmen in an effort to resist the importation of Chinese labor.

CHAPTER V

CRISPIN STRIKES

Five principal causes of Crispin strikes may be distinguished: resistence to green hands, defence of the order, opposition to wage reductions, refusal to work with non-Crispins and attempts to abolish contractors. Hostility to machinery and disputes over shop rules occasionally provoked local controversies but resulted in no really important strikes.

The green hand strikes were principally in the factories for it was there that unskilled labor could be most easily and profitably employed. Green hands were of little value to manufacturers employing hand methods. Both their "cutters" and their "makers" had to be skilled workmen.

Strikes in defence of the order were common both in the factories and in merchant capitalist establishments, in the one because the manufacturers desired to rid themselves of Crispin restraints on their employment of cheap labor, and in the other because the employers sought freedom to reduce wages. These strikes were more frequent and less successful after the winter of 1871. Manufacturers seldom succeeded in efforts to break up local lodges during 1868, 1869, and 1870, but seldom failed during 1872, 1873 and 1874.

A typical case is that of Lynn. The Lynn lodges were strong and successful in 1869 and 1870. They enforced their demands vigorously. Strikes were frequent. Manufacturers hardly dared to take orders. Some moved their factories to Pittsfield and öther New Hampshire points to escape the annoyance. Finally, in the spring of 1870, at his own suggestion, a leading employer was invited to a Crispin meeting where he proposed that a system of arbitration and wage agreements be established. The Crispins thereupon appointed a committee of five to meet a self appointed committee of manufacturers,[1] and on July 21, 1870, an agreement governing wages for the next twelve months was established.[2] A year later it was renewed, though much difficulty in carrying out the agreement had been experienced because certain employers cut under the schedule. At the end of the second year, an understanding could not be attained. The Crispins alleged "that in the spring of 1872, when contracts with the dealers were made for the next season's work, there was such sharp competition among manufacturers that they were taken at rates too low to afford the prices for labor established by the board of arbitration, and that this, more than any other cause, led to the strike the next summer and united the employers to overthrow the Crispin organization."[3]

The strike started in the trimming and edge-setting departments of thirty-five shops on account of a wage reduction of one-half cents a pair, equivalent to a loss to the journeymen of seventy-five cents a day. It soon spread to fifteen other shops and shortly involved the very existence of the order.[4]

"Matters in Lynn," wrote a correspondent during the strike, "are now in a more chaotic condition than last week, a determined war upon the Crispin organization having been inaugurated by the manufacturers who first insisted upon a reduction of wages. They have made, as a condition for employment the absolute renunciation of the order by the men. No compromise is listened to. Some prominent men are reestablishing their business in other localities more satisfactory to them. The stand so promptly taken by the employers is doubtless the result of an impression that the order is not strong enough to resist them. On the other side there is an indignant and determined spirit of resistance, especially for the reason that they are not met in a spirit of reconciliation and concession. Trade and public meetings are held and the current of feeling runs high. A retaliatory measure has been called for in the shape of an entire withdrawal of the workingmen's savings bank de-

---

[1] Massachusetts Statistics of Labor, *Report* 1877, pp. 19–49.

[2] *American Workman*, Aug. 13, 1870. "The position of affairs in Lynn, so far as mutual good feeling and understanding between employers and employed are concerned was never better than today."

[3] Massachusetts Statistics of Labor, *Report* 1877, p. 33. See also U. S. Bulletin of labor, No. 8, pp. 5, 6.

[4] *Workingman's Advocate*, Aug. 17, 1872, p. 1, c. 6.

posits, though dispassionate observers doubt whether the measure will be carried out, or if so, whether the results desired would follow. New complications of the problem are involved in the use of Hodge's new machinery for burnishing, edge setting and trimming."[5]

"It is believed that had the dispute about prices been the real question at issue, and had it been left to be decided upon its merits, the Crispins would have gained their point. It very soon became evident, however, that it was only the first move,— a mere outpost in the battle—the real object of which was to be the utter and complete overthrow of the Crispin organization in Lynn. For with this object openly avowed the manufacturers commenced to organize, funds were raised and agents sent to the several employers to enlist their aid and sympathy in the movement." [6]

The manufacturers claimed that they could no longer compete with the flourishing factories of distant towns where labor was untrammeled and cheaper, but in one shop, even before the strike started, the wage scale asked by the Crispins was offered if the men would leave the order. This they refused to do.

By the 24th of August the strike was virtually ended. The exhaustion of the Crispin treasury, the high wages offered by the manufacturers, and the hopelessness of the fight won the men away from the lodges and completely broke the organization's power. By the end of the year the last charter was surrendered.[7] In 1875 some of the Lynn lodges reorganized but without any attempt to control the green hands or to enforce a "closed shop." They were Crispins only in name.[8]

The reduction of wages was the most prolific cause of Crispin strikes and, to the average member, probably the most important. He could see more clearly the value of an organization that prevented wage reductions than the value of one which hoped, by controlling the labor supply, ultimately to increase wages. His loyalty rested heavily upon the conviction that "but for the Crispin order shoemakers would today have been virtually beggars."[9]

[5] *American Workman.* Aug. 17, 1872.
[6] Massachusetts Statistics of Labor, *Report* 1877, p. 35.
[7] Id. p. 40.
[8] Cf. Chapter VII.
[9] Massachusetts Statistics of Labor, *Report* 1871, p. 612.

Wage reductions came in three forms, "cuts," seasonal wage changes, and divisions of labor. All three resulted in strikes,[10] but those against wage cuts were the most numerous and important.[11] They occurred in every year, in every shoe manufacturing state, and in every type of manufacture, though most markedly in the shoe centers and in the merchant-capitalist shops. The latter were in a difficult situation. The factories, with their machinery and green hands, were lowering wholesale prices. The custom shops, with their individual markets, were keeping up wages. The merchant-capitalists had to meet the price-competition of the factory and the quality-competition of both the factory and the custom shop. To compete with the one they had to reduce labor costs, to compete with the other they had to have skilled workmen.

The strikes were usually provoked by employers' associations agreeing upon a schedule of wages and telling the Crispins to accept or quit. Typical instances occurred in San Francisco and Danvers in 1869. In the former city, six leading manufacturers agreed upon a scale[12] which they offered the Crispins in lieu of loss of employment; in the latter, a "ring" of manufacturers endeavored to force a lowered wage schedule.[13] In both cases the Crispins struck successfully. The issues in controversy were often more complex. The Worcester strike of 1870 is a case in point and is best described in the words of a correspondent of the *American Workman:*[14]

"Early last month the boot manufacturers of this city had a meeting, at which they adopted a schedule of prices of crimping,

---

[10] Some members, and even some locals, deprecated the attempt to force fair wages. A correspondent of this type wrote from Haverhill in 1870. "My idea is this, that more than one-half of our troubles arise from an over-zealous desire to create or maintain artificial prices for our labor. I believe the order should have nothing whatever to do with the question of prices, i. e. [wages] but return to the first principle of the order; they are broad and strike at the root and very foundation of all our difficulties, and the law of supply and demand is inevitable, and as soon as you can control one, the other can be handled with pleasure." *American Workman.* Feb. 5, 1870.

[11] Strikes for wage increases were very rare. Even the custom workmen found it a period not favorable to strikes for wage betterment. When they did strike successfully for better wage, the extra wage was taken from the consumer. cf. *Workingman's Advocate.* July 15, 19. Aug 19, 1871.

[12] *American Workman.* June 12, 1869.

[13] Same as above. Aug. 14, 1869.

[14] Jan. 29, 1870.

bottoming, siding and treeing, which is a great reduction on the prices of last summer and which they offer for the five months of winter. Besides this they require that every man who works for them shall sign a contract, according to the terms of which a man will be obliged to stay with his employer one year, whether he has full work for him or not, take his pay twice a month, with the exception of 10 days' pay, which they require to be left in the hands of the employer, thus intending to oblige an employee to forfeit whatever money may be due him if he should exercise his undoubted right of leaving his employer, whenever he deems it necessary to do so for the benefit of himself or family. The Lodge, after due consideration of the above, in a spirit of compromise and cooperation for the common interests of both, offered to submit to a reduction of 10 per cent from the first of January to the first of April.

The events leading to this strike made the refusal or acceptance of an individual contract the principal issue in dispute. But to neither side of the controversy was this the whole question involved. The employers in demanding the contracts were virtually demanding that the men give up their union, collective bargaining and the right to strike—which they knew the men would not do. The men in refusing the contract and offering to accept a 10% reduction from the first of January to the first of April were merely offering to accept a seasonal reduction and refusing all the employers really sought. The real issue involved was the union's control of the wage-bargain. The employers sought, and the Crispins refused to accede to, a return to the individual labor contract. The strike lasted three months, involved one thousand two hundred workmen and cost the Crispins in wages $175,000.[15] Its exact issue is uncertain.

The struggle which occurred in Philadelphia in January and February 1870, between thirty-one of the eighty-five manufacturers of the city[16] and the three thousand members of the Philadelphia lodges was one of the most bitter in Crispin history.[17] It seems to have been the result of a deliberate attempt upon the part of the employers to break up the unions. Their asso-

---

[15]*Proceedings*, 1870, p. 33.

[16] *American Workman.* Feb. 12, 1870.

[17] Not all of the 3,000 Crispins were on a strike but all united in directing and financing the efforts of the strikers.

ciation prepared the way for a mid-winter attack by a heavy wage cut in October. In January they demanded that the men either sign agreements to leave the order or else forever leave their establishments, hoping "by freezing or starvation" to reduce the Knights to submission. The men "scorned their offer with contempt" and left.[18] Only eight employers of the thirty-one involved were very active and of these the two largest formed the backbone of the movement. The unions, locked out even after accepting the October wage cut, demanded that wages be restored to those paid between September, 1869 and July 1, 1870. This move was as much in defence of friendly manufacturers as in advancement of their own interests. A circular letter sent to outside lodges on January 15, 1870 by Philadelphia Lodge No. 166 read as follows:

"Brethren: Some of the maufacturers of Philadelphia having reduced the wages of their men, in violation of their agreement, proposed and accepted by us last fall, and this reduction being the result of an attempt to undersell others, and take the difference in price from the wages of their men; from those manufacturers friendly to our order we have received a number of communications asking us to sustain them by compelling those parties to restore the wages of their men to the proposed and accepted rates, and thus protect them and ourselves at the same time."

The lack of unanimity among the manufacturers of the city gave the Crispins an advantage that the employers could not overcome and their effort failed. The Crispins were able to maintain their organization.[19]

A still more vigorous attack by the employers, and probably a more successful one, was that in Chicago in 1874. The Crispins had been as strong there as anywhere in the country and had subjected the manufacturer to most humiliating defeats.[20] With the waning of Crispinism the embittered manufacturers gathered themselves for a crushing assault. On the first of December, 1874, they reduced wages from 33 to 40 per cent (below the level of subsistence, according to the assertion of the Cris-

---

[18] *American Workman.* February 19, 1870.
[19] In a letter dated June 5, 1909, Thomas Phillips, Sir Knight of the Pennsylvania State Lodge at the time of this strike, says that the defense of friendly manufacturers was a principal object of the Crispins in this strike.
[20] *Proceedings*, 1869, appendix.

pins,) and locked out all who would not agree to accept the
wages offered, and not to strike, to support strikes, or to agitate
for resistance.[21]

The strikes against wage-reducing divisions of labor are well
illustrated by two that occurred in the establishment of a Jew-
ish firm in Baltimore. In July 1871, David Dalsheimer and
Son attempted to replace the "four-handed" by "string" teams.
The change would have reduced the labor cost of certain kinds
of work from four to eight cents a pair. A strike ensued which
developed into an attempt on the part of the firm to overthrow
the union. Strike breakers were twice introduced, once from
Lynn, Massachusetts, and once from Portland, Maine, but in
each case were won over and sent home by the Crispins.[22] The
second strike was precipitated by an order that the men should
"tie up" the shoes that they manufactured. It resulted in a
second victory for the Crispins.[23]

Strikes for a uniform wage through the year commonly oc-
cured in the factories. The seasonal change of wages had long
been a custom of shoe manufacture. It had been developed by
a real difference in the amount of labor required to manufacture
light weight summer and heavy weight winter shoes. At Worcester, in January, 1870, the merchant capitalist "bosses" submitted a scale of wages for the ensuing six months that was based
on this difference in the character of the work. For the three
months beginning February 1 they offered a 10% reduction from
the prices paid during the preceding five months (September
to January,) and for the ensuing three months, (May to July)
the September scale. The first period, September to February
1, was one of "winter-work," the second, February 1 to May
1, of "spring-work," and the third, May to August 1, of "winter
work" stocked up for the fall trade. It was not these seasonal
changes in wages based upon seasonal differences in work that
made most of the trouble. It was seasonal changes based on the
labor supply. The factory manufacturers paid fairly good
wages during the rush season in order to crowd the factories

[21] *Workingman's Advocate.* Dec. 1874.
[22] Same as above. July 15, 29. Aug. 19, 1871.
[23] Same as above. Sept. 7, 1872, p. 2, c 5.

with hands, then cut them 30 per cent or 40 per cent as the season began to wane. When unorganized the workmen were helpless to resist, but as soon as united into the Knights of St. Crispin they fought the practice vigorously.[24]

The adjustment of a wage scale for a shoe center like Lynn or Philadelphia was a complex task. Among the hand-work establishments the wages varied with the market supplied, the kind and quality of goods manufactured and the methods of employment. Custom shops selling directly to individual customers and at prices determined by individual bargains could and did pay better wages than retail manufacturers, wholesale manufacturers, "sweaters," or "garret bosses." Retail manufacturers could pay a little better wages than wholesale manufacturers. Direct employment, namely, the hiring of the journeymen directly by the merchant-capitalist, tended to give better wages than indirect employment, namely, the hiring by subcontractors, and also facilitated the formation of workable trade agreements. Manufacturers hiring directly could make an agreement and see that it was carried out; manufacturers hiring indirectly could hardly prevent the subcontractors cutting under the scale. The factories complicated the situation. Their machinery brought new subdivisions of labor, new measures of what constituted a day's work, and new and cheaper grades of labor. Variations between the factories in the proportion of machinery used and the manner of employing made the problem still more intricate.

The Crispin lodges included in their membership workmen from all these types of shops and from every part of the manufacture except that done by women. They therefore had to adjust with the employers proper differentials between all the different types of shops and methods of manufacturing. For this reason the agreements were always with local manufacturers' associations and specified the wages for each task in custom, merchant-capitalist and factory manufacture.

The control of the wage question rested principally in the local lodges. The International Grand Lodge never attempted to deal with it. The State Lodges were given power by the

---

[24] *Proceedings*, 1869, p. 9.

Grand Lodge of 1870 "to make laws, rules and regulations applicable to their jurisdiction concerning wages or any other matter not prohibited in this constitution, provided that any difficulty thus occuring shall be considered only a local grievance."[25]   But they never exercised their power to any considerable extent.

The Pennsylvania lodge was the only one really to take advantage of the provision. It fixed a scale of wages for Philadelphia, and a strike followed, one incident of which was the starting of a $15,000 co-operative manufacturing plant. In the same year the New Hampshire State lodge took a position in favor of uniform wages throughout the state but did not attempt to establish a scale. The New York State lodge at its meeting in 1870 urged the local lodges to assist each other in supporting wage strikes but went no further.

Nevertheless the grant of power in 1870 was significant. The national organization had begun to realize that the lack of a national wage policy was a serious defect of the national union and that some positive step toward supporting wage strikes was essential to the maintenance of the organization. This consciousness developed steadily during the next two years and at the Grand Lodge of 1872, John Dormer, International Grand Knight declared that "unless we shall be able to make some such grievance as this [reduction of wages], we will cease as an international body altogether." * * * "Such, my brothers," he continued, "I honestly believe will be our fate, unless we make provisions to support Lodges when they are fighting our battles against a reduction of wages. A reduction of wages in one section eventually means a reduction of wages all over the whole country; and still how easy it is for us to prevent all this if we only support each other against this cut-down system which is practiced upon us so often. We will then be able to fight the capitalist with his own weapon, namely, capital."[26] As a result of the discussion the grand lodge passed the following resolution and inserted it after the preamble in the Constitution.

"Resolved, that while deeming it inexpedient for this I. G. L. at this time to make a reduction of wages a grievance to be sus-

[25] *Proceedings*, 1870, p. 52.
[26] *Proceedings*, 1872. p. 21.

tained by the Order we yet consider it the greatest grievance that as shoemakers we have to contend against, and would earnestly recommend all good Crispins to aid by voluntary contributions all brothers who are struggling against a reduction of wages.''

Further development of this tendency toward a definite and national wage policy was prevented by the rapid decline of the order after the grand lodge of 1872, and the formulation of wage agreements, arbitration of wage disputes and resistance to wage reductions, remained in the hands of the local lodges.[27] These necessarily acted independently of each other (unless in the same city) and could do no more than fight for the best possible local terms regardless of conditions in other places.

Comparatively few of the Crispin strikes seem to have been for a ''closed shop.'' A few such strikes are recorded by the Massachusetts Bureau of Labor Statistics[28] and the third report of the United States Bureau of Labor,[29] but in neither case is it made clear that the strikes were for a closed shop rather than against green hands. Yet some strikes for a closed shop certainly occurred. Each local lodge had power to ''adopt such Rules or Byelaws as its own local interest may require'' [30]

---

[27] The success attained by the local lodges in dealing with wages and hours during 1869 and 1870 is illustrated by the testimony taken by the Massachusetts Statistics of Labor, *Report* 187, pp. 501, 604, 607, 611, 612. A couple of typical instances may be cited from other sources.

The Crispins of Chicago determined not to work more than 10 hours a day after January 1, 1869. (They were employed under the merchant-capitalist system.) The manufacturers were compelled to agree. As a result a correspondent from Chicago writes that "the dejected weary look has vanished, and in its place is seen the buoyant step, the glowing countenance, and the independent bearing—which make men feel they are on a par with the carpenter, the bricklayer, and the mason." *Workingman's Advocate.* Jan. 16, 1869.

Conditions in Boston where the order by the end of 1869 embraced "nearly every *skilful* shoemaker in the city" are thus pictured. "Two years ago those men were in a sadly disorganized condition, and were completely at the mercy of the employers; today the men control nearly every shop in the city, and have compelled the bosses to pay them something like living wages." *American Workman.* Dec. 18, 1869.

[28] Eleventh Report p. 28, ff.

[29] Third Report, p. 1055 ff.

[30] *Constitution*, 1869, Article VIII, p. 8.

The contractors were well described by the following testimony of a Milford contractor before a Massachusetts legislative committee: "I have been a manufacturer in Milford for some twenty-two years, and until recently never had any trouble with help. I had been out of manufacturing and out of business, and so I undertook to do some work as a laborer to get a living. I consequently got out some notices that I would run teams in my shop where and in some cases the local interest was conserved by a closed shop rule.

A much more important cause for strikes was hostility to contractors or "sweaters." [31] Their effect upon wages has already been discussed and we will now confine ourselves to the Crispin attempts to drive them from the industry. The attack was especially vigorous in New York state where strikes against "contractors or middlemen" were continuous[32] during 1870. In that year a law was placed in the State constitution, forbidding a Crispin to "make any percentage on the labor of another." [33] In 1876 the New York city Crispins, who retained a strong local organization after the national order had gone to pieces, were still enforcing this rule. Lodge No. 20, Rochester, New York, six hundred members, after three successful strikes against wage reductions, struck against and completely abolished the contract system. Similar strikes were conducted in other places. Action was taken by the international grand lodge in 1872. It added to the preamble of the international constitution the following report of one of its committees. "Your committee censure the system of a Crispin making a profit on the labor of a Brother Crispin, as contrary to the Spirit of Crispinism, but consider it impracticable for this I. G. L. to frame a law governing the case, we therefore recommend this I. G. L. to instruct subordinate Lodges to insert an article in their bye-laws suitable to their different localities." [34]

I used to manufacture. One branch of the business I thought I would take from Worcester as they were paying more than at Milford, [because their men were out on a strike] consequently I went there and took out some work, and got 20 cases to close." This work he gave out to women to close (i. e. bind) in their homes. "I don't work myself at making boots. I took the work from the manufacturers and agreed to do it for a certain price and then give it out to persons in Milford at a certain price. The difference was my profit." *American Workman,* Apr. 2, 1870.

[31] *Proceedings,* 1870, p. 16.
[32] *Workingmen's Advocate,* April 8, 1876, p. 1, c. 2.
[33] *Constitution,* Art. XV, p. 20.
[34] *Constitution,* 1872, p. 5.

CHAPTER VI

COOPERATION

The preceding chapters have shown that the Knights of St. Crispin tried to regulate wages by controlling the supply of labor and by strikes. But to many Crispins these measures were but temporary expedients. They looked to cooperation for the permanent solution of the wage problem. Their point of view was exactly expressed by Samuel Cummings: ''The present demand of the Crispin is steady employment at fair wages, but his future purpose is self-employment.''[1] From the very inception of the order this idea was embodied in its principles, provided for in its constitutions, included in its discussions, and carried out, when practicable, by its members. The preamble of the international constitution declared: ''We believe also in cooperation as a proper and efficient remedy for many of the evils of the present iniquitous system of wages that concedes to the laborer only so much of his own productions as shall make comfortable living a bare possibility, and places education and social position beyond his reach.''

Each Grand Lodge had a special committee on cooperation and in 1870[2] this committee recommended that grievance funds be invested in cooperative manufacture, under the supervision of committees appointed by the Grand Lodge, and that ''the future management of any shop or factory thus organized shall be committed to a board of five managers, elected by a committee appointed by the Grand Lodge from among the most competent and qualified Crispins in the local lodge. All profits to be disposed of as follows: 10 per cent to a reserve contingent

---

[1] *American Workman,* July 10, 1869.
[2] *Proceedings,* 1870, p. 34.

fund, 15 per cent of balance to the international grand lodge, and the balance to be divided among the cooperators.'' This was not adopted, the grand lodge feeling that it was not expedient to take the control of cooperation out of the hands of the locals.

In the same year the New York state lodge passed a resolution ''That as a remedy against the necessity of strikes, and against the evils of casual employment, of underpay for our labor and as the means of a permanent release from being placed at the mercy of those capitalists who seek to enrich themselves by taking advantage of our necessities, that this Grand Lodge recommend that the members of all subordinate lodges within its jurisdiction give the subject of cooperation their earnest attention as a preparatory means of establishing a system of cooperation in the boot and shoe business among the K. O. S. C. throughout this State.'' [3]

At the fourth Grand Lodge, April, 1871, a lengthy report upon cooperation was presented which I will briefly summarize.

I. Reasons for cooperation.

    1. There exists an open and apparently irreconcilable conflict between Labor and Capital.

    2. Labor loses forever every day's labor which is lost in striking for its rights.

II. Committee's Presentation of Plans used in Europe to Solve Wage Problems.

    1. Industrial Partnerships. Capital invested to get a certain interest, and the balance of profit divided proportionately among laborers.

    2. Cooperation, i. e. labor employing itself.

        a. Labor unions are only a means to resist the encroachment of capital. They are in themselves but an incomplete solution of the industrial problem.

        b. Cooperation in trade and manufacture is necessary for the establishment of right industrial conditions.

---

[3] *Proceedings,* 1870, p. 13.

III. Schemes of Cooperation.
   1. In general trade.
      a. Club System. No corporation, each member pays $5.00 or $10.00 which constitutes the capital and is used to make the first purchases. Sells to members at cost. Expenses have been found to average about 4 per cent and savings about 18 per cent.
      b. Corporate cooperation. Company organized with share capital. Open a store. Requires a larger capital but is superior to club. Safer and surer.
   2. In Manufacture.
    Capital of at least $200 per man required.

Two thousand copies of this report were sent out to local lodges. Many new stores and shops were formed and Samuel Cummings said in 1872 that most of them were doing well.

In the ritual for initiation to one of the degrees of the order we read: "Brothers, in order to strengthen the Order of which we are true and loyal members, and hasten the fulfillment of its final purpose, we have established these Degree Temples in order to more speedily and effectually restore the proper and natural relations between labor and capital. Experience has shown us, that while great practical good may be obtained through organizations to control the labor market, both as to supply and compensation, yet we believe the end and aim of all Labor organizations should be self-employment. With this view these Temples are formed, and all loyal and true Crispins are welcome to our ranks."

In February, 1869, cooperative manufacture was started by fifteen Crispins of St. John's, New Brunswick. By July they had one hundred and fifty members, had hired a building, put in machinery, and were planning a still greater expansion. The stock was issued at $50.00 a share and was purchasable by all Crispins, wherever located. A correspondent said, "In St. Johns, New Brunswick, the Crispins raised $20,000 and just set in motion the best shoe factory ever started there. The most improved machinery has been put into it. Offers were made in

Boston by large dealers to purchase all the goods that they can manufacture, but they were not accepted, the cooperators aiming to enter the market themselves."[4]

The New York Crispins entered cooperative manufacture in the early part of 1870. Said a correspondent to the *American Workman*:

"For the past year the Crispins of this city have talked a great deal about cooperation. The dull season, through which we are passing, has had its effect upon them; and while some were waiting for the opening of trade, others have boldly struck out to make employment for themselves, by starting cooperative manufactories. An establishment of this kind will be opened in a few days at No. 86 Warren St. with a capital of $15,000, consisting of shares at $25 each. They now have their machinery in and expect to commence work by the 10th of February. Judging from those who have charge of it, there is every reason to believe that it will be a success. A short time since, one was organized by the Germans in Brooklyn, and the members of it are now at work."[5]

The Newark Crispins started two cooperative factories during strikes, the one in January, 1873, and the other in August. The first one employed forty hands, besides its twenty members, and the second twenty in addition to its twelve members.[6]

The Pennsylvania state grand lodge passed a resolution in November, 1870, "to open a manufactory that shall belong to the journeymen of Philadelphia," and appropriated for the purpose the grievance taxes raised for the support of the dispute. In January and February, 1871, the raising of funds by sale of stock was begun. The capitalization was placed at $20,000 and the shares sold at $5.00 apiece. Over $5,000 worth of stock was sold before the end of February. The shop was soon set in operation, but the season was dull and the cooperators had to appeal to outside Crispins for aid to carry them through until the goods already produced could be sold. How long this association persisted is uncertain but it was still in business and claiming to be a "grand success" in June, 1870.[7]

---

[4] *American Workman*, July 24, 1869.
[5] Same, Feb. 19, 1870.
[6] Same, Feb. 19, 1870. Aug. 20, 1870.
[7] Circular letter.

The Monumental Boot and Shoe Co. of Baltimore was started in the fall of 1871 by the Knights of St. Crispin with a $15,000 stock divided into shares of $25.00.   They leased a three story building at 37 North Howard St., the first floor of which they used as a salesroom, the second as ''a cutting and fitting department equipped with the latest improved machinery and appliances,'' and the third as a making department.

A new note on the question of cooperative manufacture was struck by John Dormer, First International Grand Knight (First Vice President) in 1872.   He argued that Crispins engaged in cooperative manufacture should withdraw from the order.   ''My reasons are that their interests cease to be with journeymen.   I can not see any difference between a cooperative shop and a joint stock company—the cooperative men have everything to gain and nothing to lose by a strike * * * I don't want our order governed by capitalists claiming to be workmen.''   Dormer was not opposed to cooperation as such but only to the dangerous influence of cooperator-members at the lodge meeting.   He said that his position was shared by many Crispins throughout the organization who had learned by experience the evil effects of cooperation upon the local policies.[8]

Cooperative purchase of supplies and cooperative stores were even more common among the Crispins than cooperative manufacture.   In March, 1869, a cooperative association in Stoughton, Massachusetts, purchased a $2,500 lot on which they intended to build a $10,000 hall.[9]   Whether it was the plan to use a portion of the building for manufacturing and store purposes we have no record, but it would hardly seem reasonable for them to build a $10,000 hall for merely social purposes, especially at a period when wages were low and threatened to be lower.

In June, 1869, the North Bridgewater Crispins opened a store with a capital stock of $6,000 divided into six hundred five dollar shares.   Part of the officers of the association were officers of the state grand lodge and the store was one of the most successful organized in Massachusetts.   ''The principle of cooperation was fairly applied alike to stockholders and customers.   Every

[8] *Proceedings*, 1872, pp. 21, 22.
[9] *American Workman*, April 24, 1869.

store in the place marked its goods down and strong competition at once set in." Nevertheless, the sales of the cooperative store soon averaged $200 per day, and the cooperators began to prepare for cooperative manufacture.[10]

Between thirty and forty Crispin cooperative stores sprang up during the first half of 1869[11] and in the winter the Massachusetts state lodge asked the legislature for a special charter of incorporation to give them power to handle the funds of the local lodges. The charter was refused on the grounds that the Crispin purpose of controlling apprenticeship was an unlawful purpose.[12] In 1870 the demand for incorporation was renewed and through the efforts of Judge Charles Cowley and in spite of the opposition of the manufacturers, who were represented by P. Emory Aldrich, later judge of the Superior Court, was successful.[13] The purpose of incorporation was "to enable the state lodge to use the Crispin funds for buying coal, groceries, and other supplies in wholesale quantities in order to distribute them to the Crispins at prices that would lower the cost of living." The charter, granted May 26, 1870[14] contained the following provision:

Sec. 1. They were incorporated "for the purpose of managing and administering the funds belonging to said voluntary association."

Sec. 2. "Said corporation may invest any of the funds belonging thereto in the stock of any cooperative association duly organized. * * * And such subscription may be to the extent of $5,000 in any one association."

Sec. 4. "Hold property * * * not exceeding $100,000."

In the course of this hearing the limitation of the powers of the state lodges under the international constitution of 1868 and 1869 were clearly brought out. Galen E. Pratt, Grand Sir Knight of the Massachusetts state lodge testified: "We have no control over the other [local] societies. We are simply an organization formed by them for the purpose of controlling and investigating whatever funds may be placed in our hands."

---

[10] *American Workman,* Oct. 2, 1869.
[11] Same.
[12] Same, Mar. 5, 1870.
[13] *Social Economist,* July 1895. Article by Cowley.
[14] Mass., Acts and Resolves, 1870, Chap. 281.

These funds were to be used to establish wholesale coal and grocery depots and sell to Crispins at cost. ''The Legislature was not asked to endorse the principles and policy of the subordinate lodges. * * * The members of the Grand Lodge sit only as trustees, or delegates, or representatives of subordinate lodges, and the funds belong to the subordinate lodges, but are under the management of the Grand Lodge for the benefit of the whole Order.''[15]

Thus cooperation, both in the purchase of supplies and in the manufacture of shoes, formed an integral part of the Crispin movement. To it most of the leaders and a large part of the membership looked for the final solution of the problems of employment. The conflict between employers and employed seemed to them irreconcilable so long as the wage system was continued. Their ideal was, perhaps unconsciously, a return to the economic position of the colonial shoemaker, that of self-employment, ownership of the stock and direct sale to customers, individual or mercantile. The differences between the early individual shop and the proposed cooperative factories were principally in manufacturing method.

---

[15] *American Workman*, Mar. 12. April 2, 1870.

CHAPTER VII

THE SECOND KNIGHTS OF ST. CRISPIN, 1875-1878

The attempt to revive the Crispins in 1875 was in reality a distinct movement. The records of the international grand lodge held at Boston, June 11-14, 1878, show that the so-called Crispin movement of 1875 was distinct in principles, purposes and policies from the earlier and more important movement. Two of the three special committees appointed at the grand lodge of 1878, those upon arbitration and upon benefit life insurance, dealt with subjects that never, so far as shown by the official records that have been preserved, formed the subject of consideration by any committee of the original organization. The other committee, that on Laws, was the earlier Committee on the Constitution.[1]

The committee on arbitration made a report that no changes in the present laws seemed to be needed, and also submitted the following, which was adopted: "Resolved, That the Executive Board of the I. G. L. be authorized to take such action as seems proper to it to secure such legislation as may be possible in favor of legal arbitration between employer and employed."[2] The Lodge passed a further resolution "That Unity Lodge No. 32 of Lynn, Mass., be requested to lay before the Executive Board a full explanation of the manner in which said Lodge had applied the principle of arbitration, and the Executive Board shall use such explanation in the way best calculated to advance the good of the Order."[3] The Unity Lodge plan of arbitration is described in a contemporaneous report of the Massachusetts Bureau of Labor.[4] "No strike can be ordered sustained or

---

[1] *Proceedings*, 1878, p. 5.
[2] Same, p. 13.
[3] Same, p. 14.
[4] Massachusetts Statistics of Labor. *Report* 1877, pp. 41, 42.

allowed except by vote of the board of arbitration—and the unanimous consent of the shop's crew where such strike takes place.

"The board of arbitration is composed of eleven members, each from a different branch of labor, as follows: a cutter, stock-fitter, laster, McKay stitcher, beater-out, trimmer and edge setter, hand nailer and shaver, Tapley heel burnisher, McKay nailer and shaver, bottom finisher, channeler.

"They are elected to office for a year, and chosen, not alone for their integrity and general intelligence, but also because they are regarded as superior workmen, each being an expert in his branch of the business.

"The board shall have power to settle all difficulties that may arise between any member or members of the lodge and their employers, by arbitration; and it shall be the duty of the board, when such case has been referred to them, to carefully examine all the circumstances connected with it and endeavor to effect a settlement by arbitration, before giving their consent to a strike. It will not be the duty of the board to give aid or encouragement to a strike, begun without their consent, by any members of the order.[5] When any matter has been referred to the board for arbitration, it shall be their duty to appoint a committee from the board, who shall meet a committee appointed by the employer. If the committees agree upon any one plan of settlement, any decision they make shall be final." [20]

"In the thirteen months that have elapsed since its organization," says the Bureau of Labor, "this board has settled about one hundred cases of difficulty in different shops, most of them amicably and without much trouble. Nearly all of them arose from attempts on the part of employers to cut under what was considered a fair price, and as the chief object of the board is to establish and maintain, as nearly as possible, a uniform price for labor in all branches and grades of work in shoemaking, many of the manufacturers look upon the plan with favor. The smaller employers especially regard its establishment as useful and efficient in preventing ruinous competition in business."

The question of Benefit Insurance was brought up by Newell

---

[5] Same, pp. 42, 43.

Daniels at the grand lodge of 1870, but no action was taken. In the second organization it seems to have played an important part.

The movement of 1875–1878 was thus essentially distinct from that of 1867–1874. The purposes it sought, the leaders it chose, the dates of its meetings, the names of its officers, and its attitude to the labor papers that had represented the union of 1867 to 1874, all show its separateness from the earlier movement. The "green hand" principle of the first order was entirely yielded, and arbitration substituted for it. Instead of McLaughlin, Daniels, Cummings, Gavin, Wright and Mower, we find George Neal (Lynn), Joachim P. Rickard (Rochester), John H. Whelan (East Weymouth, Mass.), Charles H. Litchman (Marblehead), Gilbert Rockwood (Spencer, Mass.), and James Hennessy (Worcester), directing the policies and administration of the Grand Lodge. Charles Lichtman and James Hennessy were the only men in the second group of leaders who had attained prominence in the first organization.[6] The meetings were held in June instead of April. The Grand Knights and three Grand Trustees were dropped from the list of officers. A resolution in the grand lodge declared "That we recognize no newspaper or periodical as being in any manner the organ or the recognized advocate of the K. O. S. C., or the official medium of communication between lodges or Crispins."[7]

The three most interesting features of the grand lodge meeting of 1878 of this second Crispin organization were resolutions against "Communism,"[8] the employment by the grand lodge

---

[6] *Proceedings*, 1878, p. 2.

[7] Same, p. 14.

[8] The general attitude and purposes of this second Crispin movement are perhaps suggested by this resolution : *Resolved*, That while we demand and will exercise the right to combine for mutual aid and protection, and strive to gain recognition from our employers, upon the just and manly basis of arbitration, of the indisputable fact that there is a mutual relation between capital and labor, we wish it to be distinctly understood that we work by fair and honest means to gain our purposes. We know the sad need of union and organization among workingmen ; we realize the bitter, hand-to-hand struggle with poverty now being fought in our land by too many honest sons of toil ; we feel the oppression of the dark clouds which shadow the sacred cause of labor, and the temptation over present to make, Samson-like, a common level in a common country ; yet, with all these facts in mind, and with the firm determination to work unceasingly in a lawful way for our rights, we publish to the people our abhorrence of "Communism," and our firm ad-

of General Benjamin F. Butler to defend members of the Crispin lodge at Marlboro who had been indicted for conspiracy,[9] and an attempt to devise a "brand or stamp, to be used as a protection to the shoe craft against competition with boots and shoes made by convict labor."[10]

CONCLUSION

The Knights of St. Crispin was the first great protest of America's workingmen against the abuse of machinery. Fantastical in some of its superficial features, crude in its methods, and loose in its organization, it yet embodied an essential demand for justice. The shoemakers insisted that the benefits of machinery should be to those who toil with it as well as to those who own it or buy its products. That their effort failed, like that of most American trades, is the condemnation not of the shoeworkers but of our legal and industrial system.

---

herence to law and order. We believe our government is *a government of the people,* and that the *people,* in a day not far distant, will place upon the statute-book just laws, which will right the wrongs of labor. *Proceedings,* p. 7.

[9] Same, pp. 11, 13.

[10] Same, p. 15.

APPENDICES

APPENDIX I

CONSTITUTION OF THE INTERNATIONAL GRAND
LODGE OF THE ORDER K. O. S. C., ALSO CERTAIN
PARTS OF THE CONSTITUTION OF THE SUBORDI-
NATE LODGES OF THE ABOVE ORDER.

ADOPTED AT WORCESTER, APRIL 23, 1869. REVISED AT BOSTON,
APRIL 10, 1870; AT NEW YORK, APRIL, 1871; AT BOSTON,
APRIL, 1872.

PREAMBLE

The objects of this organization are to protect its members
from injurious competition and secure thorough unity of action
among all workers on boots or shoes in every section of the
country; claiming, as we do, that labor is capital, and the only
capital that possesses power to reproduce itself, or, in other
words, to create capital; that labor is the interest underlying
every other interest, and therefore is entitled to and should receive from society and government, protection and encouragement.

Recognizing the right of the manufacturer or capitalist to control his capital, we also claim and shall exercise the right to control our labor, and to be consulted in determining the price
paid for it—a right hitherto denied us; and believe an international organization, embracing all workers on boots or shoes
in the United States and provinces of North America is the only
way in which this right can be successfully vindicated.

We believe also in co-operation as a proper and efficient remedy for many of the evils of the present iniquitous system of

wages that concedes to the laborer only so much of his own productions as shall make comfortable living a bare possibility, and
places education and social position beyond his reach.

We therefore urge all workers on boots and shoes, in every
section of the country, to join us in this effort to secure through
the power of organization, both for ourselves and our children
after us, a steady demand and fair compensation for our toil,
and a position in society, to which, as wealth-producers and
loyal citizens, we are justly entitled.

[Your committee censure the system of a Crispin making a
profit on the labor of a Brother Crispin, as contrary to the spirit
of Crispinism, but consider it impracticable for this I. G. L. to
frame a law governing the case, we therefore recommend this
I. G. L. to instruct subordinate Lodges to insert an article in
their by-laws suitable to their different localities.[1]]

CONSTITUTION OF THE INTERNATIONAL GRAND LODGE 1869

ARTICLE I

Name

This organization shall be known as the International Grand
Lodge of the Order of the Knights of St. Crispin of North
America.

ARTICLE II

Objects

SECT. 1. The objects of this I. G. L. shall be to facilitate
the thorough organization of the trade it represents, for mutual
benefit and protection, and to secure complete unity of action
among all Lodges of this Order, subject to its jurisdiction.

SECT. 2. This I. G. L. shall be the supreme head of the
Order, and shall be the ultimate tribunal for the final settlement

---

[1] Addition to preamble adopted and ordered to be inserted in 1872.

of all trouble that may arise in or between any Subordinate
Lodges under its jurisdiction.

ARTICLE III

SECT. 1.   State or Province Grand Lodges of this Order
may be formed by representatives of Subordinate Lodges in any
State or Province where there are five or more Lodges legally
organized; and in States or Provinces, where there are less than
five, two or more shall have power to unite and form such G. L.,
or join the nearest State or Province G. L., organized as provided in this section.

SECT. 2.   All State or Province Grand Lodges legally organized as provided in section I, of this article, shall exercise general direction and control of all Subordinate Lodges which are
represented therein, subject, in all cases, to appeal to the I. G. L.
as the paramount authority.

ARTICLE IV

Membership

The I. G. L. shall consist of two representatives at large, from
each State or Province G. L., and one additional representative
for every one thousand members of Subordinate Lodges, represented in such Grand Lodge, or a majority fraction thereof.
Subordinate Lodges in States or Provinces, where there are no
Grand Lodges formed, shall be entitled to one representative in
this Lodge.   All representatives to be chosen by a majority of
votes cast.

ARTICLE V

Officers

SECT. 1.   The officers of the I. G. L. shall consist of a G.
S. K., D. G. S. K., three G. K.'s., G. S., G. T., and three G.
Trustees, who shall be elected by ballot, at each annual session
of the I. G. L., and who shall hold their offices for the term of
one year.

SECT. 2.   There shall also be a G. U., G. A. U., G. I. S., and

G. O. S., who shall be appointed by the G. S. K., at the opening of each session of the I. G. L.

ARTICLE VI

Executive Board

All executive powers of this Lodge, when not in session, shall be vested in its Executive Officers, viz., G. S. K., D. G. S. K., and the three G. K.'s, except that of altering and amending this Constitution. All decisions of the Executive Board to be subject to the approval of this Lodge when in session.

ARTICLE VII

Duties of Officers

SECT. 1. It shall be the duty of the G. S. K. to preside at all meetings of the I. G. L., and conduct the same according to the rules laid down in "Cushing's Manual of Parliamentary Practice;" examine all documents, countersign all receipts, appoint deputies of Subordinate Lodges, and see that the other officers perform their duties. He shall also call a special session of the I. G. L., in cases of emergency, or when requested to do so, by two-thirds of the State or Province Lodges.

SECT. 2. It shall be the duty of the D. G. S. K. to perform the duties of installing officers of the I. G. L., and perform all the duties of G. S. K. in his absence, and such other duties as the I. G. L. may require.

SECT. 3. It shall be the duty of the G. K. to perform the duties of the G. S. K. and D. G. S. K., in case of death, resignation, or other unavoidable cause, and render them such other assistance as they may require.

SECT. 4. All vacancies caused by the death or resignation of any officer of the Lodge may be temporarily filled by appointment by the G. S. K., or presiding officer of the Lodge, until its next regular session.

SECT. 5. It shall be the duty of the G. S. to attend all meetings of the I. G. L., and keep correct records of the proceedings thereof. He shall, under the direction of the G. S. K., notify the members of this Lodge of the time and place of meetings, of all special sessions of the I. G. L., conduct all its correspondence with subordinate Lodges; and, at the expiration of his term of office, or sooner (if called upon to do so, by order of the Executive Board), deliver up all books, papers, or other property belonging to the I. G. L., to his successor, or the G. S. K. In case of inability to attend, he shall send, or cause to be sent, all books, papers, or documents pertaining to his office, to the I. G. L., at its annual session, or at any special session. He shall perform all other duties of his office, and receive for his services the sum of one thousand ($1,000) dollars per annum. He shall also attend all meetings of the Executive Board.

SECT. 6. It shall be the duty of the G. T. to receive all moneys collected as ordered in Art. IX., pay all orders drawn on him by the G. S., when duly attested by the Executive Board. He shall keep a true and correct account of all moneys received and paid by him, and have his accounts open at all times for examination by the G. Trustees; and shall, at the expiration of the term of his office, or sooner, if called upon so to do by the Executive Board or Lodge, deliver up all moneys, books, papers, or vouchers in his possession, to the G. Trustees or his successor in office. Before entering on the duties of his office, he shall give bonds, with approved security, in such sums as the I. G. L. may determine, for the faithful performance of his duties, and receive therefor the sum of three hundred dollars per annum.

SECT. 7. It shall be the duty of the G. U. and G. A. U. to test all members at the opening of the Lodge, and perform such other duties as the G. S. K. or Lodge may direct.

SECT. 8. It shall be the duty of the G. I. S., and G. O. S., to guard the inner and outer doors of the Lodge-room, and see that no one enters without giving the proper password, without permission of the G. S. K.

SECT. 9. It shall be the duty of the G. Trustees to audit all accounts and bills; to examine the books of the G. T., and approve all bills against the Lodge, requiring at all times proper vouchers therefor; to see that all moneys of the Lodge are safely invested; to see that sufficient security is given by the

G. T. before entering on the duties of his office, and shall make an annual report of the state of the books of the Lodge.[2]

Article VIII

Rules or By-Laws

Each Subordinate Lodge may adopt such Rules or By-laws as its own local interest may require, provided such Rules or By-laws do not conflict with this Constitution.

Article IX

Revenue

The revenue of the I. G. L. shall be derived as follows, viz.: A *per capita* tax of thirty cents shall be levied on each member of subordinate lodges yearly; one-half the amount to be collected in the month of July, and the balance in the month of January, in each year. Said money to remain in the custody of each subordinate Lodge, subject to the order of the Executive Board, at any time when the Treasury may require replenishing. All money then drawn shall pass from each subordinate Lodge directly into the Treasury of the I. G. L.; but there shall at no time remain in the hands of the Treasurer of said Lodge a greater sum than two thousand (2,000) dollars.

Article X

Eligibility to Office

No person shall be eligible to office in the I. G. L. who does not represent a legally organized Lodge, and who presents a certificate of election, in accordance with Art. IV., of this Constitution; provided that this Article shall not be so construed as to render the officers of this Lodge ineligible to reëlection.

---

[2] Article VII, *Constitution* of 1872, gives the duties of officers in greater detail. A comparison of the two articles reveals many of the practical administrative difficulties met by the organization.

Article XI

On Charters

Sect. 1. All applications for Charters for subordinate Lodges shall be made through the G. S. of the State or Province Lodge where such Lodge exists, accompanied in all cases by the charter fee; and upon forwarding the Charter, the chief officer shall delegate some proper person to instruct and obligate the members of the Lodge to whom the Charter is granted, and all necessary expenses of such deputy shall be paid from the Treasury of the Grand Lodge.

Sect. 2. In all cases where no State or Province Lodge exists, application may be made direct to the G. S. of the I. G. L., and such necessary expenses as may be incurred, shall be paid from the Treasury of said Lodge.

Article XII

Time of Meeting

The annual session of the I. G. L. shall be held on the third Tuesday of April in each year, at such place as the Lodge may designate.

Article XIII

Special Duty

Sect. 1. The Officers of this Lodge, except the G. S., who shall receive only mileage and board, when on special duty, shall be allowed mileage, board, and compensation, not exceeding three dollars per day; and no officer or member shall receive more than that amount for any service performed.

Sect. 2. All expenses of offices or members of this Lodge, incurred as specified in section first of this article, shall be paid from the Treasury of this Lodge.

Article XIV

Grievances

Sect. 1. *Grievances shall consist of,* 1st. Being discharged for refusing to teach new help. 2d. Being discharged for belonging to the Crispin Organization. 3d. Being discharged for being conspicuous in organizing new Lodges of this Order, or advocating its principles.

SECT. 2. Whenever a grievance is supposed to exist in any Lodge of this organization, notice shall be sent by said Lodge to the two nearest Lodges of the Order, whose duty it shall be, when notification is received, to appoint one delegate from each Lodge, which delegates shall, in connection with one appointed from the Lodge complaining, form an investigating committee.

SECT. 3. It shall be the duty of said committee to listen to the evidence on both sides of the case, and endeavor to arrange the matter in dispute. If said matter cannot be arranged satisfactorily, it shall be referred to the State or Province Grand Lodge, where such Lodge exists; and where such Lodge does not exist, to the nearest State or Province G. L., who shall decide upon the matter, subject to appeal to the I. G. L.

SECT. 4. Whenever a grievance is entertained, it shall be the duty of the C. S. to write the G. S., stating the date of commencement of grievance, the number and names of members thrown out of employment, and the number of children under twelve (12) years of age belonging to each family. Also, the amount of money per week which it will take to supply the demands of such grievance, and to notify the Grand Scribes of State or Province, and of the I. G. L., immediately when the grievance is satisfactorily arranged.

SECT. 5. The amount paid to parties implicated in a grievance shall not exceed six (6) dollars per week for a single man; and for a man with a family, it shall not exceed, for the man, six (6) dollars per week, two (2) dollars for a wife or mother dependent upon him, and one (1) dollar for each child under twelve years of age, provided nothing shall be paid when such persons obtain employment at any other business, or refuse to engage in such employment when opportunity is presented.

SECT. 6. Each member of a Subordinate Lodge shall pay into its Treasury, fifty cents (50), which shall constitute a contingent fund, for the purpose of meeting the expense of grievances, and shall be used for no other purpose. No part of said contingent fund shall be drawn from the Treasury, except on the

[67]

order of the Scribe of the State, Province, or I. G. L.; when, on appeal, as provided in Art. V., and when such order is drawn, the money shall be sent direct to the point of grievance, and a receipt therefor shall be sent direct to the Lodge from whom the money was received; also to the G. S. ordering payment. Whenever any money is drawn from the Treasury of any Lodge, an assessment shall be immediately made upon its members, to fulfill the requirements of this section.

SECT. 7. Whenever an order is drawn for the purposes heretofore specified, it shall first be drawn upon Lodges nearer to the point of grievance, and no Lodge shall be drawn upon for more than fifty per cent. of the amount of the contingent fund belonging to its Treasury. No Lodge shall be called upon twice until all Lodges of the organization shall first have been called upon. All Lodges receiving money to sustain those thrown out of employment by a grievance, shall send a correct account of all moneys received and expended in sustaining such grievance, to the Grand Scribes of the State or Province G. L., and I. G. L., and the balance remaining shall be returned to the Treasury of the G. L. ordering the tax. Said money to remain in such G. L. Treasury for use only in similar cases of emergency. [Transferred to Secret Ritual in 1870.]

ARTICLE XV

SECT. 1. This Constitution can be altered or amended; at the annual meeting of this Lodge, by a two-thirds vote of the members present, and voting, without any previous notice of such alteration or amendment.

SECT. 2. This I. G. L. shall not be dissolved while there are ten dissenting Lodges.

Articles added to the Constitution of the International Grand Lodge at the third annual meeting, Boston, 1870.

ARTICLE IV

SECT. 2. Any Lodge neglecting or refusing to comply with orders issued by this Lodge or its Executive officers under the provisions of this constitution, or to pay all taxes assessed, for the space of three months after such orders are issued or taxes are levied, shall lose all rights to representation in the State or Province G. L., or in this Lodge, and the Executive Officers of this Lodge shall have power to take possession of Charters of such delinquent Lodges if they fail to comply with the provisions of this article, or to give satisfactory reasons for failing in so doing. Representation as provided in the first section of this article, shall be based upon the number of members not suspended in the Subordinate Lodges. [Added to the Const., 1870, on account of the difficulty experienced in collecting grievance taxes. Chap. IV.]

ARTICLE XV

Laws

State or Province Grand Lodges shall have power to make laws, rules and regulations applicable to their local jurisdiction, concerning wages or any other matter not prohibited in this Constitution, provided, that any difficulty thus occurring shall be considered only a local grievance. [Added in 1870 on account of the demands of many locals that wage strikes be supported as Grievances. See Chapter V.]

ARTICLE XVI

Eligibility of Members

SECT. 1. Any male person eighteen years of age or upwards, shall be eligible to membership, who has worked an aggregate of two years at boot or shoe making, shall bring forward evidence satisfactory to the Lodge he proposes to join, and shall at the time be engaged at his trade.

SECT. 2. No person employed as agent or foreman by a manufacturer, with power to fix the rate of wages paid, or to discharge, those employed, shall be eligible to membership in this Order, except such foremen as are employed under a Cooperative system.[3]

---

[3] Transferred from Subordinate Lodge Constitution to Grand Lodge Constitution in 1870.

ARTICLE XVII

Cards

SECT. 1.   Any member who is clear on the books, shall be entitled to a traveling card for a time not exceeding thirty days, by paying his dues up to the time to which his card extends. And upon obtaining employment his traveling card shall not be renewed.

SECT. 2.   Any member wishing to leave a Lodge and join another, can do so, if he is clear on the books, by applying to the F. S., for a transfer card, for which he shall pay the sum of twenty-five cents.   Provided, such members shall not leave one Lodge and join another in the same city or town, without the consent of the Lodge of which he is a member, also provided that this Article shall not be so construed as to prevent a member from joining a Lodge representing his branch of trade.

SECT. 3.   After receiving a transfer card, a member shall deposit the same with the Lodge he intends joining at its first regular meeting, after arriving in the place where such Lodge exists, and shall become a member of that Lodge from date of card.

SECT. 4.   No subordinate Lodge shall have power to demand a fee of a member when he deposits his transfer card.

SECT. 4.   Any member receiving a travelling or transfer card, shall be required to deposit the same with the S. K. of the Lodge nearest the locality where he may obtain employment, within seven days after obtaining such employment.

SECT. 6.   No Lodge shall have power to issue transfer cards or other documents, connected with Lodge business, without the seal of the Lodge being attached thereto.

SECT. 7.   All members shall be subject to the jurisdiction of the Lodge in the locality where they may be employed.

SECT. 8.   Persons wishing to join this organization, shall apply to the Lodge in the town or city where they reside, and if more than one Lodge exists, to the Lodge that represents their branch of trade.

SECT. 9.   Any member changing his business shall receive, upon application therefor, an honorable withdrawal card from

the order, provided he is in good standing in the Lodge and
clear on its books, and be again reinstated when he shall resume
work on boots or shoes.[4]

ARTICLE XVIII

SECT. 1. No member of the I. G. L., or of Subordinate Lodges
shall be allowed to injure the interests of a brother; such as undermining him in price or wages, or do any underhand act that
would be injurious to a Brother Crispin. Any member violating the above shall be guilty of perfidy to the order, and shall
be liable to be fined, suspended, or both.

SECT. 2. Any member violating the obligations of this order,
shall be fined, suspended, or both by a two-third vote of members present, and voting when the question is before the Lodge.
But no person shall be suspended, unless he has had a fair and
impartial hearing before a committee appointed to investigate
the charges; and such committee shall give before the Lodge a
full report of all the evidence offered in the case.

Nothing in this section shall be so construed as to prevent a
member suspended from appealing to the State, Province, or
I. G. L., for final decision.

ARTICLE XIX

The merits or demerits of any religious denomination or political party shall not be discussed within the Lodge-room.

ARTICLE XX

Any Lodge duly organized shall meet at least once a month.

ARTICLE XXI

Each Subordinate Lodge shall have power to adopt its own
Rules and By-laws, provided such Rules and By-laws do not
conflict with this Constitution, or the Constitutions of the G. S.
or P., or the I. G. L.

---

[4] The above article and the four succeeding ones suggest some of the difficulties experienced in the administration of the order.

ARTICLES ADDED TO THE CONSTITUTION OF THE INTERNATIONAL GRAND LODGE AT THE FOURTH ANNUAL MEETING, NEW YORK, 1871.

ARTICLE VI

SECT. 2. It shall be the duty of the Executive Council to decide all questions and appeals arising between State, Province or Subordinate Lodges. They shall keep a true and correct account of all subjects referred to them for decision. They shall draw all orders on the treasury, subject to approval by the Trustees, requiring at all times a majority of each board to transact business.

ARTICLE XIII

SECT. 2. Delegates to the I. G. L. shall be allowed mileage, and for time and expenses to and from the I. G. L. at the rate of five dollars per diem.

ARTICLE XVI

SECT. 3. Any person presenting a clearance card from the Amalgamated Cordwainers' Association of Great Britain shall be received free of charge.

CONSTITUTION OF THE INTERNATIONAL GRAND LODGE OF THE ORDER OF K. O. S. C., BOSTON, 1872.

Resolved, That while deeming it expedient for this I. G. L. at this time to make a reduction of wages a grievance to be sustained by the Order, we yet consider it the greatest grievance that as shoemakers we have to contend against, and would earnestly recommend all good Crispins to aid all brothers by voluntary contributions who are struggling against a reduction of wages.

ARTICLE VII

Duties of Officers

SECT. 1. It shall be the duty of the I. G. S. K., to preside at all meetings of the I. G. L. and conduct the same according

[72]

to the rules prefixed to this Constitution; examine all documents, appoint Deputies to Subordinate Lodges, in accordance with section 11 of this article, and shall receive the sum of $200 per annum in full for all services rendered while on duty, provided this article shall not be so construed as to deprive him while on said duty for this Lodge of his mileage and board, and in no case can he charge this Lodge with expenses incurred while visiting a Subordinate Lodge or Lodges, said Subordinate Lodge or Lodges requiring said visit to pay all expenses. He shall see that all officers of the I. G. L. perform their several duties, and shall also call a special session of the I. G. L. in cases of emergency or when requested to do so by two-thirds of State and Province Grand Lodges.

SECT. 2.   It shall be the duty of the I. D. G. S. K. to perform the duties of installing officers of the I. G. L., and perform all the duties of I. G. S. K., in his absence, and such other duties as the I. G. L. may require.

SECT. 3.   It shall be the duty of the I. G. K. to perform the duties of the I. G. S. K. and I. D. G. S. K., in case of death, resignation, or other unavoidable cause, and render them such other assistance as they may require.

SECT. 4.   All vacancies caused by the death or resignation of any officer of the Lodge may be temporarily filled by appointment by the I. G. S. K., or presiding officer of the Lodge, until its next regular session.

SECT. 5.   It shall be the duty of the I. G. S. to attend all meetings of the I. G. L., and keep a correct record of the proceedings thereof. He shall, under the direction of the I. G. S. K., notify the members of this Lodge, of the time and place of meeting, of all sessions of the I. G. L., or its Executive Council, at least thirty days before said meeting takes place; conduct all correspondence between this I. G. L. and Subordinate Lodges. He shall submit to the State, Province and Subordinate Lodges, on the first days of May, August, November, and February, a quarterly report, in which he shall set forth the condition of the Order in regard to the state of business, number of members, standing of Lodges, number of members in the different localities within the jurisdiction of this I. G. L. He shall furnish to

[73]

the Subordinate Lodges suitable blanks for the proper compilation of the information required. He shall in all cases when a State, Province or Subordinate Lodge fails to comply with the requirements of Article 8 of their Constitution, notify the Executive Council thereof, and if they fail to comply with the provisions of Section 2, of Article 4, their Charter shall be withdrawn. He shall, at the close of his term of Office, or sooner if called upon to do so by orders of the Executive Council, deliver up all books, papers or other property belonging to this I. G. L. to his successor or the I. G. S. K. In case of inability to attend the meeting of this I. G. L., or the Executive Council, he shall cause to be sent all books, papers and documents pertaining to his office, to the I. G. L. at its annual session, or at any special session, and perform all other duties pertaining to the office of I. G. S., and shall receive seven hundred dollars, per annum.

SECT. 6. It shall be the duty of the G. T. to receive all moneys collected as ordered in Article 9, pay all orders drawn on him by the I. G. S., when duly attested by the Executive Board, and approved by the Board of Grand Trustees. He shall pay no bills except approved by a majority. He shall send to the I. G. S. a report of the financial standing of the I. G. L. Treasury, showing the standing of all Subordinate Lodges on the Books of the I. G. L. on the first days of April, July, October and January. He shall receive for his services the sum of three hundred dollars per annum.

SECT. 7. It shall be the duty of the G. U. and G. A. U. to test all members at the opening of the Lodge, and perform such other duties as the G. S. K. or Lodge may direct.

SECT. 8 It shall be the duty of the G. I. S. and G. O. S. to guard the inner and outer doors of the Lodge Room, and see that no one enters without giving the proper pass-word, without permission of the I. G. S. K.

SECT. 9. It shall be the duty of the Board of Trustees to approve all bills or orders presented to them by the Executive Council when found correct. But they shall in no case approve any bills or orders, unless accompanied by the proper vouchers.

They shall keep a true and correct account of their transactions in office.

SECT. 10. At the opening of the annual session of the I. G. L. there shall be elected an auditing committee of three, whose duty shall be to investigate the reports of the Executive Board, and audit the accounts of the I. G. T. and I. G. S.

SECT. 11 Each Lodge shall have one Deputy, who shall be appointed by the I. G. S. K., through the I. G. S. of the I. G. L., upon the recommendation of the Lodge for which he is to act, whose duty shall be to install its officers, receive and communicate the pass-word to the S. K. or K., when acting in his absence; collect and forward all taxes levied by the State, Province or International Grand Lodge before installing its officers. All moneys collected by the Deputy shall be at the risk of Subordinate Lodges, and said Lodges shall at all times implicitly comply with the orders of the Deputy. Any Deputy failing to comply with the requirements of this Article, shall be deemed *guilty of perfidy to the Order and liable to suspension.*

And in case he faithfully performs his duties his term of office shall be from the time of his appointment until the next session of the I. G. L.

CONSTITUTION OF THE SUBORDINATE LODGES OF THE ORDER OF KNIGHTS OF ST. CRISPIN, 1869[5]

ARTICLE VI

It shall be the duty of every Member of this Lodge who employs or works with or for a person not a member of this order, to use his utmost endeavors to induce such person or persons to join the same.

ARTICLE VII

Every member who employs help in the making of Boots and Shoes, shall employ men who are members of this order provided the quality of workmen who are members, requisite for his service can be obtained.

---

[5] Local lodge constitutions were framed by the International Grand Lodge.

CONSTITUTION OF THE SUBORDINATE LODGES OF THE ORDER K. O. S. C.

ARTICLE X

New Help

No member of this order shall teach or aid in teaching any part or parts of boot or shoe making, unless this Lodge shall give permission by a three-fourths vote of those present, and voting when such permission is first asked. Provided this article shall not be so construed as to prevent a father teaching his own son. Provided, also, that this article shall not be so construed as to hinder any member of this organization from learning any or all parts of the trade.

ARTICLE XIV

There shall be a committee appointed, known as the Vigilance Committee, whose duty it shall be to prevent, if possible, any violation or infringement of the obligation, Constitution, or By-Laws, and to report everything of this character before the lodge, said Committee to consist of as many members as the lodge may determine.

ARTICLE XV

In case of the death of any member of this lodge the S. K. shall call a special meeting, and it shall be the duty of the members to attend his Funeral in full Regalia.

ARTICLE XVI

Any member of this lodge having decided to become a manufacturer shall give notice thereof at the next regular meeting, when, if he is clear on the Books, he shall be suspended provided, that if he return to journey work again he shall be reinstated to all the privileges of the lodge by complying with its Laws.

RITUAL OF THE DEGREE OF * * * IN THE ORDER
OF THE KNIGHTS OF ST. CRISPIN, TEMPLE OF
* * * BOSTON, 1870

OBLIGATION

You each and all solemnly and sincerely pledge yourself, your
sacred word and honor, that you will, under no circumstances,
divulge any of the secrets of this Temple to any person whom
you do not *know* to be a member of the Temple of which you
are a member, and whose standing is good (except your religious confessor); that you will not make known any signs,
pass-words, tests, or any other work of the Temple. You also
pledge yourself to bear true and faithful allegiance to the Order
of the Knights of St. Crispin, and obey and enforce its constitutional rules and obligations, to the best of your power and
ability, by all proper means; and you also agree to do all you
can to persuade all true and loyal Crispins to join this Temple,
and unite in this work of protecting and elevating labor. All
this you promise freely of your own accord, and without any
mental reservation whatsoever. You also agree to be governed
by the will of the Temple expressed in the manner provided in
the Constitution. This obligation you agree to keep inviolate,
as long as these Temples exist.

All this you promise, on honor before God and these witnesses,
who will bear swift witness against you should you prove false.

APPENDIX II[1]

FROM THE THIRD ANNUAL MEETING OF THE INTERNATIONAL GRAND LODGE OF THE ORDER OF KNIGHTS OF ST. CRISPIN, IN BOSTON, MASSACHUSETTS, APRIL 19–30, 1870

"* * * The suggestion that I wish to make first, is, that all claims for grievances should be settled by the International Executive Council, and not by the State Lodges, for this reason, there are certain localities where they consider that it is right to make a strike a grievance. If there is a State Lodge in that locality, and they being composed of the members of that locality, would of course be in favor of turning a strike into a grievance. And then there are localities where a strike could not be recognized as a grievance, and I might add that hardly any kind of a difficulty could be recognized as a grievance; therefore, I say, let all of those claimed grievances, go to the International Executive Council, and they being composed of persons from all of those different localities, they will work for the interest of all, and consider and settle those difficulties strictly in accordance with the requirements of the International Lodge. The next is, with regard to the duties of Deputies. Last year, when the business of the session was about at an end, in order to be liberal and just with the Lodges, I proposed to them, that they select a brother for Deputy, and that I would give him an appointment, with the understanding of course that any one delegate who represented a Lodge was considered its Deputy. This method of procedure does not give importance enough to the office, and I know it to be most essential to the well-doing of the Lodges. Therefore, I suggest

---

[1] This appendix presents typical addresses made by K. O. S. C., Grand Lodge officers at International Grand Lodge meetings. They show the state of the order and the viewpoints of the officers.

that certain questions be laid down in the constitution for the proposed Deputy to answer by communication to the I. G. C. S., as soon as he is selected by the Lodge. I will give you a sample of the questions that I would ask. "What are the purposes of our organization?" "What method do you think would be proper to adopt in order to accomplish those designs, and yet work in accordance with the fundamental principles of the order?" "What are the fundamental principles of this order?" "Do you understand the responsibility that a brother takes upon himself in accepting the position of deputy?" Have you read section first of Article VII of Subordinate Constitution?" The working out of the answers to these questions would have a tendency to fit him for the office, and it would give the I. G. S. K., an idea of his competency, and if he was not competent to the task, he should not be appointed. I would suggest that you amend Article VII, section twelve, of the Subordinate Constitution, so that the deputy will understand that he is responsible to the I. L., for the action of his Lodge; responsible to this extent, that he shall notify the I. G. C. S., if his Lodge does not live up to the requirements of the I. G. L., in every direction. That it shall be his special duty to see that all taxes are paid as soon as they become due, and that he shall communicate to the I. G. C. S., the condition of his Lodge at least once in two months. And that the section alluded to, should be the first one in the Article in place of the last. That the I. G. Lodge should bestow some token of respect upon any deputy who serves the International Lodge faithfully through one term, but if his Lodge is a delinquent, he will have to prove to the International Lodge that he has done all in his power to bring them up to constitutional requirements.

You perhaps think it strange that I dwell so much upon the duties of deputies, but after I explain, you will see the necessity. At our last annual session we had some evils to overcome which were great obstacles to the well-doing and carrying on of the institution. The greatest of these was that some of the Lodges were perfectly indifferent with regard to the payment of the International and Grievance taxes. While the Chicago Grievance was going on, there were certain persons who discouraged

[79]

the Lodges from sending in their taxes. It is very easy to discourage individuals from paying out money, so easy that one man wishing to get the good will of the majority, can baffle a dozen of good men from sending any money to the International or suffering Lodges. I want the deputies to know their duties, and do them. I want them and the Lodges to understand that they have their authority from the International Lodge, and that the Lodges must obey and respect them, particularly when they remind them that they are doing those things which ought not to be done, and leaving undone those things which ought to be done. The deputy and officers of a Lodge should confer together, to promote the interest and welfare of the Lodge and its members; not to connive for self-aggrandizement, as has been the case, I am afraid, too much already, for I know of Lodges where just before an election of officers or delegates, certain jealous mischief makers would connive together and poison the minds of the members against the officers. I actually know where the question of opposing the use of machinery has come up three or four different times, just before an election, and it has been used as a lever to hoist them into office, or keep them in for another term. We want no such conniving; it is not manly. It is dishonest, yes, rascally. We want they should reason together, so that they can work together in Harmony, to promote the greatest amount of good to the greatest number. I sincerely believe that if the deputies had understood their duty, and the Lodges had known their power, all the Lodges who have had recognized grievances would have received the money due them at the proper time, which has not been the case. Many persons have said to me, "are you not discouraged." My answer invariably has been, "No, sir." Well, they would say "I am. I think the order never saw such trying times. We are terribly in debt, and no money to pay it. The plan of keeping the money in the Lodges is a failure." And they would go on to tell how the members of the International Lodge did very wrong in adopting such a plan, that they might have known better, etc. Let me say, brothers, it is very easy for us to say that anything is wrong after it has been proved to be so. It is very easy for us to say that a certain measure is wrong after we have tried it for one year, and it has proved to be a failure. But let me say that this idea of having a contingent fund in the Subordinate Lodges, *is a good one.* I believe that there can be no better plan for the safe keeping of the money, and that it can be sent to any point where a grievance may arise as soon as from two to ten days after the grievance has been recognized. The machine is right, but the operators are wrong. Let me just cite to you briefly the manner in which this department has been managed. When the C. S., of a Lodge receives notice of the recognition of a grievance, and that his Lodge is called upon to send a certain per cent of their contingent fund in support of it, he puts the communication into his pocket, and forgets all about it, till after the meeting, and if the Lodge meets but once a fortnight, it will be in his possession about three weeks before the Lodge knows anything about it. He then brings it into the Lodge and reads it, it may be acted upon, and it may not; if it is, you will find perhaps a member who goes against everything that is brought up, unless it may be something for his benefit. If they propose to give him the Deputy or Sir Knightship, or want him to go as a delegate to some convention, he will not say one word against it. But as soon as the communication is read, he will make a motion to lay it on the table, that there is so much business to be done, that it cannot be attended to. If he does not succeed in tabling it, he will tell them that they do not know about this grievance. The Executive Council or the State Officers may not have done right in recognizing it. That he does not know that the money will be properly used. So he goes on in this way, while the men whom he pledged himself to support are suffering, perhaps for something to eat, for the support of a principle which is to benefit every brother in the order. If the members of the order knew that the deputy had power to stop or reprimand them for talking against any requirement of the International Lodge, they would not attempt to do so. I do not say this to make you think that the rank and file are not right, for never did I see men so faithful to any cause, as they have been to this; they could not be more faithful to the country or friends. And we have a National reputation to that effect which we cannot afford to lose. But I say that the whole trouble lays in the officers; they do not attend to their duties; the first thing for the officers to do is to see to it that the Contingent fund is collected; this once done and the rest is perfectly simple and easy. When an order comes for grievance money, it is the duty of the officers to see that the money is sent immediately. It is not necessary to bring it before the Lodge; it is a Constitutional requirement; the Lodge has nothing to do with the money; it belongs to the International Lodge; it is simply kept there for safe keeping. In consideration of those facts, I would therefore recommend that if the deputy is absent from two successive meetings, that he be obliged to communicate the fact to I. G. S., and give his reasons for being absent. This will have a tendency to make him attend the meetings, which will assist the Lodge very much. And if he cannot prevail upon the Lodge to come up to the requirements of the International Lodge, he should notify the I. G. S., immediately. I would amend the constitution so that the deputy would be the person to receive the order, and when he received it, that he could present it to the Treasurer immediately and receive the money; so you see there would be no delay with regard to the sending of the money. And it should be required of the S. K., that he should cause to be read all documents issued from the International Lodge at least three different meetings. I want this specified, because the reports from the International Lodge have not been read properly.

*   *   *   *   *   *   *   *   *

Last International session we found ourselves in debt about ($20,000) twenty thousand dollars. The Executive Council cleared up all the apparent mysteries of the Chicago grievance, so that all the delegates were perfectly satisfied. They all promised to go home to their Lodges, and if they were in arrears to induce them to send the money right along to pay Chicago; but the money did not come. Why not? I answer, because the rank and file did not understand it. The delegates did not take pains to push the matter. At the meeting of the Executive Council, held in October, the Council took into consideration the question of delinquent Lodges, and came to the conclusion that it would not be just for them to levy a tax upon the Lodges that were not in existence at the time of the Chicago grievance, neither did they think that it would be just to ask the Lodges who had paid their dollar and twenty-five cent tax, to pay it over again. And neither did they expect that they would pay any assessments for those grievances until the delinquent Lodges were obliged to pay. We knew that we had no power to force these Lodges to pay their taxes. So, there was nothing left for us to do but to ask each member who had a heart in this institution to contribute voluntarily one dollar or upwards, for the purpose of paying our debts; debts that were contracted in fighting our battles. But there has been very little money received on that call. California sent $252.46. That speaks well for Crispinism in California, although they were not in existence as a Lodge at the time the debt was contracted, yet they had heart enough in the institution to help pay its debts. Now, I firmly believe if the officers of the Lodges had made an effort to collect the money on that call, we would not be in debt one cent today. I will venture to say that there is not one-third of the members of this order who knew anything about that report. I do not believe that half of them ever heard it read. I have been to many Lodges where they would ask me many questions with regard to the state of the International Treasury, and in order to answer them correctly, I generally referred to the Council's and Treasurer's report, and they would enquire with surprise what book that was and why they could not have one, and on enquiring I would find that the officers forgot that they ever had received one. I tell you these men should be stirred up, they must have deputies that will follow them up close and make them do their duty.

*   *   *   *   *   *   *   *

WM. J. McLAUGHLIN, I. G. S. K.

REPORT OF I. G. SCRIBE

*   *   *   *   *   *   *   *   *

We have assembled for the third time as a National Body. Our first meeting July, 1868, at Rochester, New York, was for the purpose of organizing a National Union of our Craftsmen, and to make such laws as were deemed best for the welfare of the organization. The whole thing being then an experiment. The laws that were there made must of necessity be an experiment also.

At our second meeting in Worcester, Massachusetts, in April, 1869, with the experience of the past ten months as a guide for our future management, we were then prepared to make improvements in our laws, which was done I think to the satisfaction of all at that meeting.

But as time moves, our experience increases with our age. We now find our past year's experience tells us our laws are still imperfect, and need improving.

During the year I have issued one hundred and twenty-three charters (123) thus making in all three hundred and twenty-seven (327). These charters are not quite all filled, as I have allowed several of the State Grand Scribes to hold blank charters to be issued by them whenever the occasion required, to save time.

During the year there has been organized nine State and Province Grand Lodges, thus making in all eleven, in the following States: Massachusetts, Wisconsin, Maine, New York, Pennsylvania, Illinois, Ohio, New Hampshire, Michigan, Indiana and Province of Ontario.

The Executive Council have been called together once during the year. Their deliberations have been printed, and a copy sent to each Lodge.

Grievances during the year, have been numerous, extensive, and in some cases very destructive to the Order, for the reason that they are not promptly and sufficiently supported. I think in most cases where there is a grievance the Lodge becomes to a certain extent demoralized and discouraged, and is seldom as flourishing after.

This is one of the most important things to be considered at this meeting. These grievances must be better attended to, or we shall soon have no organization.

The constitution seems to provide plainly and effectually for grievances, but notwithstanding all this, in its practical operations, it must be considered a failure. Lodges do not collect the contingent fund in many cases until it is called for, and then they cannot, for our grievances come in almost every case in winter, just when most of our men are out of work, and of course then it cannot be collected.

I have had many letters substantiating this fact, and further, there are too many that have power to draw on the contingent fund, so much so that it is next to impossible to keep the matter straight, and know just where we stand.

Every State Grand Scribe and the I. G. S., have power to draw in case of a grievance, and no Lodge is allowed to be drawn on but once, until all others have been, and no Lodge shall be drawn on for more than fifty per cent of the contingent at a time.

And now, to illustrate. Our first grievance was in Quebec, I commenced to draw on Lodges for fifty per cent of the contingent fund to go to Quebec, and among the rest I called on several of New York Lodges, when to my astonishment after so doing, and just at that time I found there was a grievance in Binghamton, and that Bro. Wells of New York State Lodge had drawn on some of the same Lodges that I had, and had only drawn for fifteen cents of the fund. Here it will be seen that Lodges in New York had been drawn on twice, and others none at all, this was a violation of the constitution, though no such was intended.

Again, I was drawing on Massachusetts Lodges, and found there, that Bro. Cummings and myself had come in contact with each other. Finally all Lodges have been drawn on twice, for the fifty per cent of the contingent fund except in New York State where they have been drawn on twice as the constitution provides but for only half of what the other Lodges have been. No wrong was intended, but after making one mistake there seems to be no way to correct it.

Our State and Province Grand Lodges are now so numerous, that it seems to me proper for this body to adopt some plan to prevent International and State Lodges coming so often in contact with each other, it is discouraging to both officers and members. I have had much complaint in this direction. I think the International Lodge should have nothing to do directly with the Subordinate Lodges where there is a State Lodge, but that all orders, etc., from I. G. Lodge should pass through the hands of the State Lodge, and thus give us a more perfect system of working.

*   *   *   *   *   *   *   *   *

I wish to call the attention of this body to Article IX, Sec. 3, in regard to eligibility of membership, in relation to foremen and manufacturers. I think this section should be materially changed, modified, or more clearly defined. In several places in the Western States where the manufacturing is confined to custom work, Lodges have got into some trouble with the manufacturer, and their best and leading men have been obliged to leave town or open a shop of their own. The cases are quite numerous where members have opened a little shop of their own, have been obliged to leave the order as soon as so doing, which has been detrimental to the Lodges and weakened it very materially. From the commencement of our organization, I have never been able to see the necessity of asking a member to withdraw from the order because he happens to be fortunate enough to rise to foremanship, or even start a little business for himself. I contend it does not follow that a member cannot be a good member still under these circumstances as long as he is willing to be governed by our laws. When we get good men, I believe it is our duty to keep them if we can. We need more good men than we already have. I would go as far as to allow a custom manufacturer to join the order. For, if they join they must comply with our rules. If they do not join, there is nothing to prevent them from teaching new help as much as they please. It should be borne in mind that our western custom manufacturers are very different from those of the East, where it is more in the line of wholesale. They are all practical men or nearly so, and are fully qualified to teach new help which is the very thing we are trying to prevent.

* * * * * * * * *

Again, Article X of Subordinate Constitution, should not be inserted in the constitution; it is enough to have it in the Ritual. I believe it is another reason that retards our progress in obtaining State Charters.

The Article allows any Subordinate Lodge to grant a privilege to any of its members to teach new help. I believe this should not be. No one should have such privilege, except the very highest authority, and then even only in extreme cases.

Our Lodge in Quebec is in a very low condition indeed, the men are persecuted for being members of the order, and they have even asked me to give them an honorable discharge and let them go. I am not able to suggest any plan for their relief. At the time of their grievance they were in bad shape; but Bro. McLaughlin went to their assistance and succeeded in doing them a great good. He also went to St. John, and succeeded in restoring that Lodge (which had almost ceased to live) to a healthy and active condition. The Lodges in the State of Maine I understand are badly off, having lost nearly all their interest in the order. I have had very few communications from them.

* * * * * * * * *

Very few of our grievances have been fully paid, which has greatly discouraged the members in those places. This must be overcome. By taking some measures to fully relieve ourselves from such embarrassments, we can do it if we will, and must. We must not only pay what we already owe; but we must prepare for next winter, though I do not think we shall have so much to contend with next winter as we had in the past.

GRIEVANCES

The grievances in Quebec continued nine weeks, and cost as first reported the sum of $3,472.78; amount received was $1,085.35; balance due $2,387.43. Since this report was received the Lodge has received more money, and I am not able to say precisely how much is their due at present.

The grievance in Binghamton, New York, in September, was referred to New York State Lodge, and declared such by said State Lodge. The cost of which was the sum of $585.50; amount received was $637.30, thus leaving a surplus of $51.80, which was returned to the State Lodge.

Grievance in Newark, New Jersey, which was a large affair, and was recognized by New York State Lodge, is not fully paid, and I cannot give the amount their due at present. The Lodge had a great deal of trouble among themselves during this grievance, in consequence of some dissatisfaction arising between the members and the Corresponding Scribe.

Grievance in Philadelphia as recognized by Pennsylvania State Lodge, was also a large affair, and is not fully paid. The cost of the grievance and the amount now their due I am not able to give.

Georgetown, Ontario, grievance recognized by Michigan State Lodge, continued five weeks, with thirteen married men and six single ones, and twenty-eight children. Cost of which was $745.00; the amount received was $121.65, leaving a balance their due of $623.35.

Grievance in Prescott, Ontario, as recognized by New York State Lodge, I am not able to give the amount of cost, nor the amount they have received.

Grievance of James Hennessy in Detroit Lodge No. 26, as recognized by Michigan State Lodge; continued three weeks, and cost the sum of thirty dollars.

Grievance of Henry Hamill in Lansing Lodge, No. 316, as recognized by Michigan State Lodge, continued three weeks, and cost the sum of thirty-three dollars.

Grievance in Ashland Lodge, No. 12, recognized by Massachusetts State Lodge, the cost of which was $82.50, which is not paid.

Grievance in New Bedford Lodge, No. 128, as recognized by Massachusetts State Lodge, the cost of which was $1,300, they received $1,000, and the amount their due is $300.

Grievance in Lynn, as recognized by Massachusetts State Lodge, not able to give the figures.

Grievance of James Bills, of Albion Lodge, No. 283, of Michigan, and recognized by Michigan State Lodge, the cost of which was $12. Whether they have received the amount or not, I am not able to say.

This makes during the year twelve grievances.

The old grievance of Chicago Lodge, No. 7, total amount of cost, $35,898.98; amount received, $12,539.36; balance due, $23,359.62.

Milford grievance is not yet paid; the amount their due I am not able to give.

I have received during the year for Charters, Constitutions, &c., the sum of $793.82. I have paid out during the year for printing, stationery, stamps, &c., the sum of $388.36; leaving a balance of $405.46 now in my hands.

NEWELL DANIELS, I. G. S.

FROM PROCEEDINGS NEW YORK STATE LODGE, SECOND ANNUAL MEETING, HELD IN SYRACUSE, N. Y., APRIL 5TH, 6TH, 7TH AND 8TH, 1870

Resolutions Upon Prison Labor Passed by New York State Lodge in 1870.

WHEREAS, The workingmen of this state, in convention assembled, recently framed certain laws intended to ameliorate the condition of all classes of laborers, and presented the same to the Legislature for consideration; and

WHEREAS, The promises made by many of the members of that body that the Bills in question should be placed upon their final passage without delay would seem to have been made only to have been broken; and

WHEREAS, We consider the Bill for the better protection of the mechanics of this State, by regulating the use of convict labor is a measure which, if passed, will benefit all classes of society, but more especially the large number of men known as the Knights of St. Crispin; therefore be it

Resolved, That the present system of contract for prison labor is injurious to us as workingmen and subversive of our best interests as citizens; we demand that the same shall be at once and forever abrogated by the passage of the Bill now under consideration in the Senate, as passed by the Assembly in its entirety.

Resolved, That we, as workingmen, will use our best endeavors to defeat any candidate for office who shall hereafter be placed in nomination by any of the existing political factions who shall so far forget our interests or ignore our rights by not acceding to our just demands that the aforesaid Bill be passed.

Resolved, That a committee of three be appointed, whose duty it shall be to prepare a record of the names of the members of the Senate and Assembly who shall vote for or against the bill, and have a list of the same printed and posted conspicuously in every workshop and other places of resort throughout the City and State, that workingmen may know how to treat them, as friends or foes, when they again present themselves as candidates for our suffrages.

Resolved, That the Contract System of Prison Labor is directly and indirectly opposed to our interests, and that we should use every effort to remove the obnoxious evil.

FROM PROCEEDING OF FIFTH GRAND LODGE, BOSTON, APRIL, 1872

PROCEEDINGS

Fourth Day—Afternoon Session

*　*　*　*　*　*　*　*　*

"There is another point which I wish particularly to call your attention to, and that is the learning of new "Help." W e may all consider that necessary to our welfare, but there are many circumstances which demand that this objection should not be tolerated, as for instance the learning of the orphan of him who died in his country's cause, as also the learning of the children of other Trade Unionists, who may fancy our craft. These considerations I earnestly recommend to you; also, the advisability of abolishing State Lodges, as I consider, under existing circumstances, they are not needed.

*　*　*　*　*　*　*　*　*

I. G. S. K, *and Brothers:*

For the fifth time in the history of our Order, and the third time in Massachusetts, has assembled the representative Crispins for the purpose of comparing notes and taking counsel for the future. Before entering on a discussion of the general matters of my report, you will permit me to allude to some matters of a personal nature. When the present administration (to use a convenient phrase) entered upon their duties, they did so under very discouraging circumstances. In the first place, the whole Order was sadly demoralized by influences beyond our reach or control, and therefore we were at first in a measure moving in the dark. From enemies within and without, there seemed to be danger that another session of the I. G. L. would never be held, and even some of our true men held that opinion; but our Executive Officers being of that class who believe that any just principle will in the long run assert its supremacy, decided to issue an address to the Lodges, setting forth the changes that had been made in the policy of the Order at the session of 1871, and under their instructions I issued a circular bearing date of April 30, 1871, which I am happy to say met with a friendly response from the Lodges.

In the second place, we had a treasury heavily in debt, and to no one was this so serious a trouble as myself, owing to the failure of parties who held my entire available means; but, through the kindness of Bro. Mower, I was able to get through safely. His kindness will never be forgotten. Again, I was unable out of the materials transferred to me to make, in an intelligent manner, the annual reports without calling on Bro. Ryan for assistance, consequently he came on from New York, and together we succeeded in arranging the annual report, which was issued at the earliest practicable moment. If there was delay in issuing the usual reports, it certainly was not the fault of the officers of the I. G. L. As soon as received from the hands of the printer they were at once sent to all the Lodges known to be in existence. We did not issue any reports in any language other than English, for the simple reason that we saw no means to pay the large expense it would incur. So much I have to say in the way of explanation of matters the Lodges may not have understood.

I now pass to the consideration of the quarterly reports required by the Constitution on the first days of May, August, November and February. I may be liable to censure for failing to issue these quarterly reports, but I beg leave to remind you that had I done so on the days required, the exhibit would have been such that I fear you would not have been called together in session today. Experience teaches us that our weakness ought never to be exposed even to our friends; and so meagre were the returns received by me that I chose rather to run the risk of censure than to discourage the weak Lodges by any exhibit of our apparent weakness. Do not infer from this that I regard the Order as in a state of decay or likely to go down. By no means; but that I simply wish you to understand that the Lodges are so tardy in sending in their returns that, had I strictly complied with the provisions of the Constitution, I fear there would have been few Lodges now in existence. Deal with me as you choose, but I feel sure that I have acted for the best, and time will justify the truth of my assertion. You will also recollect that at the last session a preamble and resolutions were adopted, addressed to our fellow craftsmen in England, urging them to organize under our plan. I caused, early in June last, to be neatly engrossed a copy of the above, together with a letter from myself, as I. G. S., and directed the same to Mr. George Dadsham, Secretary of the Amalgamated Cordwainers' Union of England, to which no reply was received. So, again I had another copy engrossed by an expert penman on the 27th day of November, 1871, and also inclosed the following letter to Mr. Dadsham:

BOSTON, MASS., November 27, 1871.

MY DEAR MR. DADSHAM: Last June I sent you a copy of the inclosed Preamble and Resolutions, in which you will perceive that our desire is to unite under one head all the members of our craft on both sides of the Atlantic. We are not selfish in this desire nor do we desire in any way to interfere with your own internal arrangements, but simply to come into closer relations with our brothers in England. Please let me know as early as possible what action may be taken by the honorable body of which you are the Secretary and oblige your most obedient servant and fellow worker in the cause,

S. P. Cummings, I. G. S.

Of the International Grand Lodge of the Knights of St. Crispin of the United States of America and the Canadas.

To George Dadsham, Esq., London, England.

To this letter there has never been any response, so we must infer that these letters failed to reach their destination, or else the craftsmen of England do not care to organize under our plan.

* * * * * * * * *

Of Charters I have issued during the year 18, located as follows: Massachusetts, 3; Pennsylvania, 3; Rhode Island, 1; New Jersey, 1; New York, 2; Tennessee, 1; Missouri, 1; Illinois, 1; Province of Ontario, 1; Province of New Brunswick, 1; for which I have received the sum of $225. I have had great difficulty in getting out Charters, owing to circumstances beyond my control. At the time I assumed the duties of my present office, I received from my predecessor eighty-five Charters, all of them signed by the former I. G. S. K., and no means of printing any new ones. So I had to consult a chemist as to how the name could be erased. Nearly every attempt was a failure at first, because of leaving a stain. I have filled all orders for them, though I have blundered in numbering them.

I now desire to offer you some suggestions drawn from my own experience during the past year. I think we should have prepared a careful digest for the use of our Lodges, explaining as far as possible the meaning of the different Articles of the Constitution. In all other Orders, such as the Masons, Odd Fellows, Good Templars and others, digests are used, and many a trouble has been amicably settled that threatened to become serious. Why should we not have one? An Order like ours, composed of such diverse elements, liable at any moment to come into collision with each other, makes a digest an imperative necessity; and, in my judgment, were such a book or pamphlet put into the hands of every Lodge Deputy, containing full instructions and explanations, one half our present troubles would be avoided.

*   *   *   *   *   *   *   *   *

Last April you adopted a lengthy report on the all-important subject of co-operation, and ordered 2,000 copies printed for the use of the Lodges and as a public expression of your views. I had them printed as soon as possible and sent them out to the Lodges and the press. The report was fully reviewed and commended in several papers, and I think, have a good public impression of the Order. Since April last several new co-operative shops have been started and are doing well, so far as I hear. Of clubs and stores there has been an increase, and only one has given up the ghost. I am still of opinion that co-operation is the true solution of the industrial labor problem, and hope to see it become general among the members of our Order.

As I pass to the condition of the Order both as to numbers and moral strength, I wish to emphasize all I have said in the preceding pages in the way of suggestions, and hope they may receive careful and friendly consideration. In the way of returns, if they are the only criterion by which we are to be judges, we are very weak:

For July 1, 1871, the whole number was 13,715. Good standing, 6,237.

For October 1, 1871, the whole number was 12,926. Good standing, 4,677.

For January 1, 1872, the whole number was 13,779. Good standing, 6,584.

For April I make no report as very few returns have as yet come in. Thus, you see that my information is not very favorable, so far as numbers are concerned, and I still think I acted wisely in not issuing the facts to the Lodges as many of them were struggling for life, and any discouraging information might have ended them. January 1st shows the best for the year, and I think April will show still better. Passing to the concluding topics of my report, I must say that I have no fears for the future of this Order, because it is founded in necessity and justice, and cannot die until the one is removed and the other forgotten.

Finally, Brothers, what is to be our future? Are we going up or down? Shall we grow weaker or stronger? Five years have passed since seven men organized the first Lodge. Since then it has become International as a Union, and has a world-wide reputation; but after all its battles and victories, its struggles and sacrifices, what has it accomplished? Accomplished! It has more than lifted into respectability the craft it represents; it has forced forward the discussion of the labor question a quarter of a century in five years! I have traveled largely over the country the last three years, mingled with lawyers, politicians, clergymen and editors, many of them with world-wide reputations, but never yet seen the hour when I was ashamed to say, "I am a Crispin." The Crispin Order has wielded for five years the most powerful weapon avarice, love of power and selfish greed ever met, and though sometimes the weapon may have been turned aside or blunted, still, in the number of its battles and its victories, the Crispin Order stands without a peer on the Continent. We know labor has been better paid, better respected, become vastly more intelligent because of our existence; we know how today labor and its rights is the absorbing topic of public and private discussion—all this the work of five years.

S. P. CUMMINGS, I. G. S.

*   *   *   *   *   *   *   *   *

"Again we have come together for the fifth time in the history of our organization to devise ways and means whereby we may be able to solve this problem, that is, how can we, as shoe-makers, maintain our present rate of wages, or in fact increase the price of our labor, which I know some parts of the country are sadly in need of at the present time. No doubt but that there are many members of this convention who think, while we provide against the admission of new help, that in time we can control the price of labor, or, in other words, sell our labor for whatever we please. To those who hold such views I will refer

them to the history of trades unions in Germany, France and
England, and you will see this curtailing the surplus help is
nothing new with us. In fact, it is as old as trades unions themselves; it has always existed, and I trust it always shall exist,
but in a different form than we have it at present in the
Crispin Order. I am well aware there are those who are opposed to making any innovation upon what are considered the
fundamental principles of our Order. However, I am satisfied
in my own mind that the time is not far distant when we must
adopt some law for apprentices; for I claim it will be more to
our advantage to learn the youth of our country than to have
foreign nations do so for us. Now, what benefit shall we derive
if we should never learn another shoemaker in this country? To
my mind this question seems plain enough that we would gain
but very little by such a course of action, for European markets
would then become the school of instruction for the future shoemakers of America. Now, if all trades adopted our rule in regard to help, in another generation there would be no such
thing as an American mechanic in the country. I suppose the
question will be asked, If the prevention of new help does not
maintain the price of our labor what will? That, I think, is
the question foremost in the minds of many of our members at
the present time, and that is what I have often asked myself,
and I have arrived at this conclusion: that in order to restore
confidence to the minds of our members we shall have to convince them that it is for their interest to belong to such an Order
as this. Now, how shall we be able to convince them that they
will be benefited by a union of this kind? I would say, make a
reduction of wages a grievance, then every member will feel
that he has something to lean upon in the hour of his adversity.
I feel confident, myself, that, unless we shall be able to make
some such grievance as this, we will cease as an international
body altogether; and I would, in all sincerity, ask of the delegates present, aye, and every shoemaker in the country, what do
you think would be the consequences then? Why, simply this:
for a short period of time some of the Lodges would have a
local existence, and disappear like the dew drops on the hillside
before the morning sun. Such, my brothers, I honestly believe

will be our fate, unless we make provisions to support Lodges
when they are fighting our battles against a reduction of wages.
A reduction of wages in one section eventually means a reduction of wages over the whole country; and still how easy it is
for us to prevent all this if we only support each other against
this cut-down system which is practiced upon us so often. We
will then be able to fight the capitalist with his own weapon,
namely, capital. I hold that without money we can never expect nor need we hope to be successful. In fact, without money
we have about the same chances of being successful with a capitalist as an unarmed mob would have to defeat an armed and
well disciplined army. I trust this grievance question will receive due consideration from every delegate present, for upon
this depends the life or death of our Order.

There is also another subject I wish to call your attention to:
it is what is known as Co-operation. Now, I find during the
last year the minds of many of our members have changed in regard to allowing members to own shares and work under what
is known as the co-operative principle. I feel inclined to think,
myself, that, for the safety of the Order and best interests of
the many, it would be well if the men holding shares and working in co-operative shops should withdraw from the Order. My
reasons for urging this are these: When any number of men
join together and succeed in establishing a trade, their interest
ceases that moment with the journeymen. I cannot see any difference between a co-operative shop and a joint stock company;
and then, again, it might so happen that the co-operative member would be the means of inaugurating a strike in order to
throw the other men out of employment, and thereby decrease
the number of shoes in the market. The cooperative members
would have nothing to lose by a strike, but, on the other hand,
they would have everything to gain, because they would con-
tinue to work and the price of their shoes would increase, which
would add to their profits. I do not wish it to be understood
that I am opposed to co-operation; far from it. Indeed, I would
do all I possibly could to encourage the spirit of co-operation
among our members; but I don't want to have our Order governed by capitalists claiming to be workingmen. However, I

feel satisfied that co-operation has not yet attained that magnitude but what we can control it.

*   *   *   *   *   *   *   *   *

When I obeyed the summons of the I. G. S. K. and met in Baltimore on the 28th of August, 1871, I found the I. G. S. without his books, so, therefore, I could gain but very little information in regard to the condition of our organization. At that time I protested against the way subordinate Lodges were neglected by the I. G. S., and he promised the Council in future he would be more prompt with his correspondence, but it has been the same old story ever since. Lodges keep complaining they can receive no communication from the I. G. S.; in fact, the matter came to such a crisis that on the 9th of October last I wrote to the I. G. S. K. and demanded the removal of the I. G. S. from his office. This statement I merely make to defend my action in regard to the I. G. S. during the past year. I think also that, as a piece of economy we owe to the Order at large and to expedite the workings of the I. G. L., we should consolidate the office of I. G. T. and I. G. S., and feel confident such a change would benefit not only the I. G. L. but subordinate Lodges also, as they could send their reports and taxes to the same office, and would also prevent subordinate Lodges from getting the password when in arrears; but the way the I. G. L. conducts its business at present any Lodge in arrears is liable to receive the password, for the I. G. S. has not the means in his possession of knowing how the Lodges stand on the books of the Treasurer, and therefore sends the Lodge that may be in arrears the password. I hold it is our duty to make such laws that will prevent Lodges in arrears from receiving the password and thereby protect Lodges in good standing. I would suggest that there be some law enacted in regard to those members that have gone to work in prisons, for I believe we have nothing in our laws at present that alludes to prison labor; therefore I consider this a very important subject for your consideration. I would also call your attention to the fact that about two-thirds of what were once Crispins have ceased to pay any dues, and to all intents and purposes have left us. Now, we all know that this is a deplorable state of affairs. The question is, how can we restore our Order to its former strength? I am afraid, myself, this is rather a difficult question to answer. There is but one way that I can see how we can accomplish this object, and that is to grant an act of amnesty to members in arrears. This, I think, would have a good effect; and if we can succeed in getting those delinquent members back again, we may possibly be able to retain them, because we have experience from the past five years which will be a guide for our future, and will not lead us into any visionary measures.

JOHN DORMER, I. G. K.

APPENDIX III

The purpose of this appendix is to give a few facts in regard to the meetings, officers and other internal history of the Knights of St. Crispin.

MEETINGS OF THE GRAND LODGE

1. Rochester, N. Y.   July 1, 1868, 87 lodges represented.
2. Boston, Mass.   April 20–27, 1867, 133 lodges represented.
3. Boston, Mass.   April 19–30, 1870, 133 lodges represented.
4. New York City.   April, 1871.
5. Boston, Mass.   April, 1872.
6. Philadelphia, Pa.   April, 1873.

PRINCIPAL GRAND LODGE OFFICERS

International Grand Sir Knight
    1868–71.   Wm. J. McLaughlin, Ashland, Mass.
    1871–72.   Thomas Ryan, New York City.
    1872–73.   Jas. P. Wright, Baltimore, Md.

Deputy Grand Sir Knight
    1868–69.
    1869–71.   Richard Griffiths, Chicago, Ill.
    1871–72.
    1872–73.   Jas. Hennessy, Chicago, Ill.

Grand Scribe
    1867–71.   Newell Daniels, Milwaukee, Wis.
    1871–72.   Samuel P. Cummings, Lynn, Mass.
    1872–73.   M. P. Murphy.

Grand Treasurer
    1867–68.   Newell Daniels, Milwaukee, Wis.
              (in connection with his work as Secretary.)
    1868–73.   Chas. C. Mower, Upton, Mass.

First Grand Knight
    1868–69.   Martin Gavin. Chicago, Ill.
    1869–70.   J. B. Upham, Elmira, N. Y.
    1870–71.   Jas. Hennessy, Chicago, Ill.
    1871–72.   John Dormer, St. Louis, Mo.
    1872–73.

At the Grand Lodge of 1870 the *American Workman* of Boston was made the official organ of the order while the Chicago *Workingmen's Advocate* was approved as a proper representative in the west. In the same year the New York State Lodge chose the *New York Tribune* as its state organ. In October, 1872, the first number of the "K. O. S. C. Monthly Journal" was published but it ran through only a few numbers.